Ex Libris

_____

_____

This book is
dedicated to
all the people
who have made
Grandiflora what
it is today.

Saskia Havekes

This book is
dedicated to my father,
Paul, without whose
influence and
encouragement I would
never have picked up
a camera.

Andrew
Lehmann

Grandiflora
Celebrations

SASKIA HAVEKES

PHOTOGRAPHY BY ANDREW LEHMANN

LANTERN

an imprint of

PENGUIN BOOKS

Contents

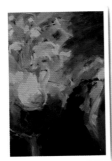

INTRODUCTION

Grandiflora has expanded in every aspect since I started the business. Comparing our Christmas party in our first year with last year's party says it all. Our first Christmas party consisted of four of us having a lunchtime picnic in Sydney's Royal Botanic Gardens under an enormous Bunya pine tree: my partner Gary; my business partner at the time, Eva Seltner; John Ladyman, who helped us design the interior of the shop, and me. By contrast, last year's party was an 'event': thirty people – staff and partners – with a massive paella cooked by Danks Street Depot chefs, and a belly dancer with a carpet python snake.

We're now into our second decade. The actual shop is still the same, but there's now a lock-up storeroom, an ever-expanding office and the storage area in Darlinghurst. Grandiflora has become a tight-knit family, and we often see more of each other than our own families. Actually, our families are often involved, as this is a very hands-on profession with a lot of room for extra help. The business has developed a life of its own. I often see it as a ship in waters that are sometimes troubled, sometimes calm, sometimes up against enormous odds, with many people on board, with petal sails, bamboo struts, ropes of twine and a tug to pull the flower-laden barges.

The very tiny shop and workspace houses us all, and the flowers of course, as well as a steady stream of tradespeople and customers amid the ever-present buzz of the phones. We shuffle around like pieces in a jigsaw puzzle; it's all 'Excuse me' and 'Sorry, sorry'. It would be interesting to have a camera on the ceiling on a busy day and replay the footage to see how we all manoeuvre around the large workbench that is its centre. My ancient family crest exhibits the word, 'Fortitudine', which sounds old-fashioned – it's Scottish, and means 'fortitude'. I have found I need a lot of this to face every day with all its challenges.

My jobs now also include much larger events and I've had to learn to cope with extremely long hours – all the events photographed in this book took place over just one and a half years. My stepfather, an ardent admirer of the poet Louis MacNeice, sent me this:

Leaving Barra
Who as yet have only an inkling
Though some facts foster that inkling –
The beauty of the moon and music
The routine courage of the worker,
The gay endurance of women.

And you who to me among women,
Stand for so much that I wish for,
I thank you, my dear, for the example,
Of living like a fugue and moving.

For few are able to keep moving,
They drag and flag in the traffic,
While you are alive beyond question
Like the dazzle of the sea, my darling.

I was touched by the observation and the fact that someone else could understand the reality of what I do.

Recently I was asked, 'What is your creative process?' For me, it is layers and layers of experiences and thinking that meld together and form a resource that I can call upon. It's pretty spontaneous, really. I don't do any drawing; I'm not very good at it. When I have more time I'd like to develop that skill. People often ask for my sketches of a job but I've usually got it pretty clear in my head — I guess I 'sketch' in my imagination and articulate the image in real space.

I get a lot of inspiration from the markets and from nature in general – the raw materials suggest the way forward. Inspiration also comes from bush walks and botanical gardens, especially when I travel. I love to go to markets and botanical gardens in other cities in Australia and all over the world. I particularly enjoy Vita Sackville-West's famous garden at Sissinghurst in Kent, England, influenced 'by Vita's love of the floral arrangements of the Dutch masters, their abundance and romance' (Tony Lord, *Gardening at Sissinghurst*). That's where it comes from – a bit of osmosis, saturation in the vegetation and the passion. The Spanish poet Federico Garcia Lorca calls it 'duende', loosely translated as 'soul'. I also love Bangkok's night markets, where monks in saffron robes walk through endless stalls of marigolds, enormous bundles of lotus flowers and people creating leis and intricate jasmine adornments for brides.

Inspiration comes from other places too. My mother's camphor chest has always been filled with beautiful clothes and fabrics of the past, the elegant 1920s and 1930s eveningwear of her mother, my grandmother, Sybil Marguerite Russell, who made a chaperoned trip to 'the Orient' in the 1930s. She brought back beautiful kimonos with motifs of peonies and chrysanthemums on silk fabric. I loved taking them out and imagining how the world was then. There's also my father's pottery; I watched shapes emerge from the clay as he worked on his potter's wheel and admired the beautiful glazes he produced: many variations of blue, deep and dark, rich and strong or pale and subtle, sometimes with a bronze glaze. And my great-grandmother, Dorothy Frances Macrae, was such a flower-lover she could have been named after Saint Dorothy, patron saint of florists and gardens. I like to think so.

In the early, early morning I go off in my cantankerous van to shop for raw material to create something beautiful. It's just me, the van and the sunrise, and the sky turning the colour of the flowers: rose pinks and sun yellow, orange and red. The Sydney flower market, full of energy and action, is the lifeline to the raw material we work with. I go personally twice a week, but we shop there for Grandiflora three times a week. There are lots of little pockets of special things that you have to look for; you have to know the market well enough to know who will have the sort of thing you need. Many specialties are set aside for good customers. If the growers know you well enough they'll keep special items for you rather than putting them out on the stand.

It's a very local industry; Australia imports only a few tropical things such as antheriums. That's the beauty of our market: it is quite home-grown, not perfectly manicured. I love the Sydney flower markets and really look forward to the seasonal changes throughout the year. Also, building relationships with private growers can be very satisfying.

These people always follow their passion, and there are plenty of flower addicts who love their produce. Without these people we can't go forward. I thank them all and have included a page on some of our main growers in this book.

We frequently install onsite, so work doesn't often come out of the shop already assembled. With weddings and large events we often take everything to the venue and completely create the occasion onsite, but not always. I know many florists don't; they do everything offsite and then transport it to the venue. For me, it makes a difference because the creation is then completely bespoke to the environment. It's got a different energy, giving real life to it; it reflects the way I feel when I work. It feels more like painting, looking for different shapes and colours, composing, often layering.

I am keen to link up with other creative people to workshop ideas. I find teamwork stimulating whilst following a brief from beginning to end. My colleagues and I work really well as a team; I come up with an idea and we all add to it. We've got such a strong connection now that when we go into the job we don't need to talk to each other much; as an example, Sean usually knows he'll be up the ladder, with me directing him from the ground. I found that really difficult in the beginning, I sort of felt I was being condescending but it's essential to work like this.

Grandiflora has grown to see us doing events I would never have dreamed of. For example, we've had the opportunity to work with Jeff Leatham, an American known as 'the rock-star florist of the world'. Grandiflora supported him flower-wise with our team while he was here doing a floral installation for the Four Seasons Hotel in Sydney. At the time he was also organising the floral concepts for a huge wedding in France. He asked if some of us wanted to help! So three of us went, and it was an amazing experience, especially observing how he works. It was challenging, the job being over four venues, but looking back I learnt so much, especially watching how he managed his teams.

We shopped at Rungis, the wholesale flower markets in Paris, which are very beautiful and ever so French. The buyers walk around with their woven cane baskets and beautiful old wooden trolleys. A lot of woodland twigs, green foliage and moss that we don't have in Australia are sold there. They seem to colour-code everything; there are stands where there are purples only, then another section with all white flowers, another with only yellow and so on. It has a huge sundries section, just for ribbons and vases, three times the size of our whole market – I was overwhelmed by it all. Jeff said, 'Goodness, if you think this is overwhelming, wait till you get to Holland.' Aalsmeer, the enormous flower market in Amsterdam, services most of Europe and many other parts of the world.

I've had wonderful opportunities like that where people have believed in me enough to ask, 'Can you do this?' and that's how I've learnt to be open-minded. I often feel like I don't have much choice; I'm very driven. I always feel like a tightly stretched elastic band but maybe that's part of the creative process, having that tension – for me it is. It's just important to be mindful not to let it get too out of hand, utilising tension to push you forward into a creative spell – it's satisfying when that happens. Everyone dovetails in and pulls together and that's really productive – I wouldn't be here if I didn't have that passion for this vocation.

I want this book to be a 'mood board', an inspiration for people's own creations. Plants and flowers have a central place in my heart, and flower-lovers will know exactly what I'm talking about. You miss them when they're gone: from a vase, from a room, from a garden. They give so much. I hope this book serves as a lasting reminder of some of our creations, and will inspire you to create your own.

Life in Abundance

Warm air shimmers
the crush of heat
petals crimp and stamens crisp.

Trees toss, branches drop, doors slam:
the southerly hits.

One of the most unusual birthday gifts I think I will ever receive is from master chef Kylie Kwong. It's a lunch for twelve, cooked by her, at home. Needless to say I am astonished! Some other special occasions are also being celebrated, and Kylie and I decide to collaborate. It's taking me quite a while to absorb and start organising. The look is to be 'A life lived in abundance', with generous food, flowers and friends gathered together in an architectural space. I dream of summer flowers – lotus, frangipani and waterlilies nestled in vases from the colourful Dinosaur Designs Sun Range.

The appointed day turns out to be exceptionally hot. Sydney temperatures are up to 40 degrees but this is what I do and what I am, so we carry on. Oh, and we have a wedding to complete beforehand. 'Wilt' is the forbidden word. We try to keep the food and flowers cool for as long as possible, spraying and fanning, reciting Buddhist words of kindness.

Fifty lotus leaves, some almost a metre in diameter, and their accompanying flowers, are picked by rowing boat from the growers' pond in Glenorie (an hour's drive across Sydney) and delivered straight to the doorstep in Bronte, arriving precisely on time. But they have dried out, crisp and crumbling like biscuits. My mouth hangs open: the lotus flowers are crimped around the edges and spotted brown from the heat. We try some of the leaves in the tall vases down the centre of the table as envisaged, and watch as they curl and shrivel. Time for Plan B. Their understudies are 'elephant ears', another large green leaf. Also down the length of the table are about thirty different-sized vases, each containing a small orchid or specimen of some sort. It's a carpet of colour – a golden sunset theme paying homage to the sun.

'I'm worried that you haven't eaten all your mushrooms.' Kylie's concern for others shines through as she looks down the table to check. Towards the end of lunch, a southerly buster hits – a great wind followed by teeming rain. It's a relief after the day's stifling heat. The house has been shut up all day to keep out the heat; now we open everything to let the cool air in, but the wind slams the doors and windows shut again. We look out to sea and watch the storm as it rolls in.

I've been working with Steve, our lotus grower and a former florist, for ten years but this was the first time I'd been out to see his property. Believe it or not, this photo is real – we were holding on to the stems and using them to pull ourselves through the water. They were packed very tightly – a forest of stems.

Varieties grown include 'Hindu' and 'Mrs Perry Slocum'.

The lotus is important as a prayer flower in Buddhism. It signifies eternal life, as well as purity, because the flower rises unblemished above the mud in which it grows.

The round, flat leaves with their radiating veins look very shapely dried; they are sculptures in their own right.

I love this photo — it really brings out the contrast between the Australian bush and the rich green carpet of lotus leaves.

Lotuses

It has taken the dam years to produce the lush growth you can see here. Water levels shouldn't fluctuate too much — the leaves only grow to a certain height, so if the dam is flooded and the leaves are underwater for too long, they'll drown.

Doilies &
Pearls
Oysters & Shells

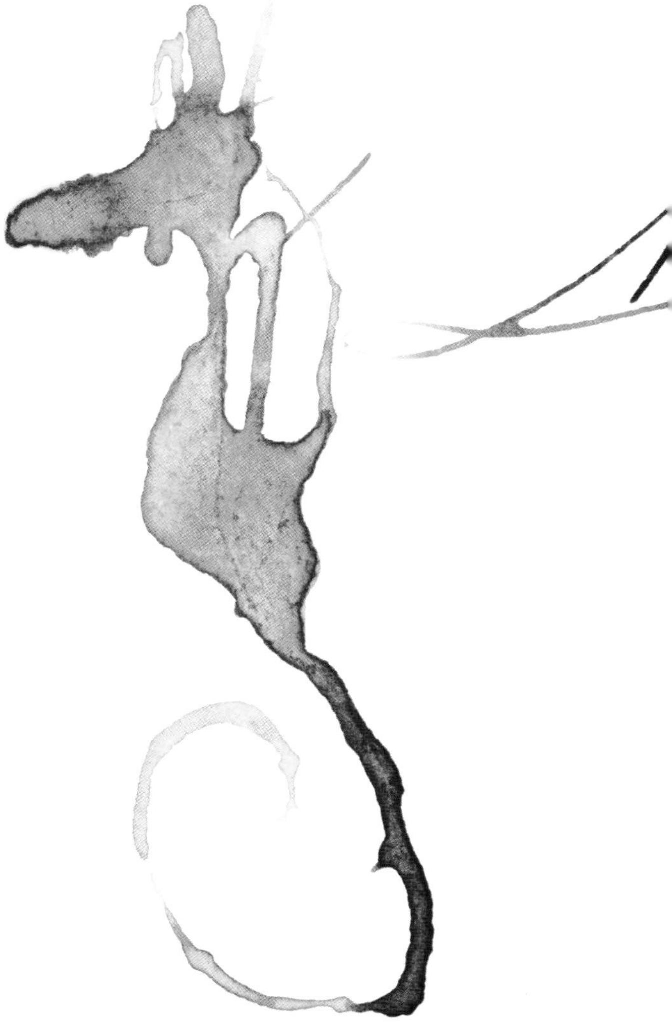

I saw this nest when I was visiting a photographic studio one day and asked to borrow it for the shop. Now it's the centre piece for this fashion parade.

This cascading waterfall of bracken fern echoed the seaweedy-looking fabric on some of the models' dresses.

The invitation to Romance Was Born's fashion show reads:
'The sea inspires tales spun from the Antediluvian age before Atlantis sank to her briny resting place at the bottom of the ocean. We sail through time, when the mythical creatures of the seven seas were ruled by mighty Poseidon and his kingdom of Nereids.

'A time when beautiful sea nymphs and Aphrodite reigned supreme. Come and swim with Romance Was Born amidst iridescent jellyfish, sea horses, schools of fish and dancing electric eels . . . but beware, deep below the waves where shy oysters and ivory shells hide, a seaweed monster lurks . . .'

This is a very intense job because of the time constraints – we need to be at the venue, The Wharf Restaurant at the Sydney Theatre Company, at 4.00 a.m. as the parade starts at 9.00 a.m. It works like clockwork, which is unusual for the fashion world. We have done the Kit Willow show (see page 83) the night before, so we're already feeling quite stretched.

We have worked in the Sydney Theatre Company many times, especially the restaurant area. The focal point is a giant nest, six feet in diameter. We hoist it up into the ceiling and it becomes the central structure for this show 'in-the-round'. We make a large cascading waterfall of green bracken fern and green amaranthus (to give the look of seaweed), as well as flowers, that flows down to the floor, then up on to the main table and back down on the floor again. An enormous central arrangement

of old-fashioned flowers – especially plumbago and rosehip – sits in the centre of the table amongst the greenery.

The theme is 'underwater with a bit of granny', so I charge around the markets saying to my florist friends and growers 'I'm shopping for granny today'. All I can think of is mauve, carnations, babies' breath and anything that we don't normally buy. I like doing this, just to challenge the brain a bit. There is one cluster of carnations that really stand out for me, a really unusual orangey-brown colour, and there are quite a few outfits that, when placed next to this cluster, work brilliantly – a really unexpected combination.

Other objects, supplied and installed by art director Mark Vassallo, include giant seahorses, nautical rope, twigs, branches, sand and sea shells. All these things are supported and threaded between a base of chicken wire lashed on to a central column and strapped with cable ties to the nest, and we take a lot of plants out of their pots, exposing their roots.

I make a huge headpiece for one of the models. I can see everyone backstage standing back, saying 'Whoa, that's a big one, is she going to fit through the door?' I don't think they are really expecting that she will. I've done similar headpieces before and it's taken years of experience to get them right structurally – I know it will be fine. As the model stands in the centre of this massive installation, a 'rainforest sprite', with her headpiece towering over the bejewelled octopus on the central table, I see it all come together, very much a team effort.

Epiphany

We relish being given carte blanche for a job; it gives us a sense of freedom and a huge capacity to invent. In this case, the client is a designer and creative director, and a close business associate of Grandiflora. We were delighted that he asked us to do his wedding, especially as he is happy to take our lead and be totally surprised on the day (although he will be involved in some of the planning).

A wedding in the forest is mysterious and unpredictable! The ceremony will be held in a park and the reception at a city restaurant. We have created a number of wedding ceremonies outside in the elements, so we know how much planning is involved – we'll need to work out of the van, using it as a mobile workshop. We have to make sure we have everything, and be very organised with secateurs, wires, cable ties, saws, buckets, floral foam, vials, ties, ribbons – the list is endless.

We rope in Greg, our flower courier, to make trips to the park with further loads and to be a taxi service to those running between the locations for the ceremony and the reception.

There is no master plan for the forest location: I have to use my intuition, deciding as I go, thinking on my feet. The ambience in the forest is very inspiring: dappled sunlight alternates with overcast cloudy shade, and the pine trees on the hill provide dark silhouettes. The couple pick a large, leafless, shiny tree, rather stark, to be married under – the only non-pine in the area. We create a long entrance path, scrabbling around the forest floor clearing pine cones so no one stumbles. We replace them after the event, covering our tracks. We place potted flowering pansy plants at irregular intervals, surrounding them with a nest of undergrowth and pine needles. There are candles and white rose petals to indicate the way for the bridal party. All this is done at very high speed with every available pair of hands helping; we have a lot of ground to cover in a very limited time.

For the bride's bouquet we tie together five long-stemmed, fully fluffy white peonies with ribbon. We actually make her five bouquets to choose from and suggest the ones she doesn't use could be put in vases around the family home where she will be getting dressed. To decorate the 'marriage tree' we create attachments of coloured hydrangea, massed together, strapping them on in a lower fork of the tree, and another around the base, ending on the ground with the white rose petal path from the forest.

For the reception, we cannot have flowers on the narrow dining table as there is only room for candles and tableware. Instead, we decorate the bar with tight clusters of nude-coloured roses and white hydrangea, and small bunches of cyclamen and peonies. The restaurant is small, intimate and elegant with smoked mirrors; on the ceiling is an enormous but not very sturdy circular 'chandelier', approximately 3 metres across, and painted soft pink. The manager is most concerned about the weight of the flowers we intend to decorate this feature with.

We do a lot of workshopping to find a solution for the chandelier. We anguish over it; everywhere we go, the worry of it goes with us, 'What to do? What to do?' Eventually we hit on the idea of creating paper flowers from light, thinner-than-thin tissue and tracing paper, alternately threading in skeleton leaves by the thousands. We need plenty of extra nimble fingers to help with this, as well as threading them onto long strands of fishing wire with individual white Singapore orchids and plucked pieces of green hydrangea. These are then tosssed over the chandelier structure. It is a lovely, ethereal result.

Afterwards we peer in from the street to admire our handiwork and are joined by a group of emos, who ask if they could have the same for their own wedding.

A Tower of Teacups

There was a table set out under a tree in front of the house,
and the March Hare and the Hatter were having tea at it:
a Dormouse was sitting between them, fast asleep, and the
other two were resting their elbows on it, and
talking over its head. 'Very uncomfortable for the Dormouse,'
thought Alice; 'only, as it's asleep, I suppose it doesn't mind.'
Lewis Carroll, 'Alice in Wonderland'

I n the Victorian era when *Alice in Wonderland* was written, teatime usually took place in the late afternoon. The party to which Alice was not formally invited was actually a very sombre affair, not like this merry afternoon. The March Hare presided over an enormously long table laden with cups, saucers, jugs and plates, dwarfing the four guests. Hot tea, and bread and butter were the only refreshments.

We are creating a much cheerier Mad Hatter's Tea Party using beautiful objects created by Edit, a showroom with wit and true originality.

To establish a floral theme for this event, we look at the items in the collection. Many of the objects contrast sophistication and whimsy.

They are placed around a large rectangular glass table and have a truly timeless feel. They have been created for modern living but still evoke previous eras.

The objects are placed around the table. We arrange fragrant roses in the eclectic range of vases. The small, precious clusters of individually picked flowers add an emotive potency. For a Victorian look, we put hydrangea under a glass bell jar. By the time we've finished, it feels as if the sleepy dormouse could appear at any time, followed by the Mad Hatter.

Serena, our hydrangea grower, is something of a pioneer,
running the family business at a time when it was quite
unusual for women to do so. I have watched the business
grow to become a much larger operation.

Hydrangeas need protection from the elements;
some are grown under gigantic gum trees, but
the greater proportion of them are grown under
a shade cloth. This shade cloth was a huge
investment and there was lots of excitement
when it went up.

The different colours are due to
the acidity or alkalinity of the
soils - acid soils produce blue and
purple flowers and alkaline soils
produce pinks and reds. Serena lets
some of the large white ones grow
until they become what's known as
'antique hydrangea', a specialty
of hers. These are really big and
green, flecked with burgundy.
Sometimes they are picked on long
stems and dried.

Three generations of hydrangea growers: Serena, her
father, and her son. This is the quintessential family
shed! It's their bunching room, where leaves are plucked
and the flowers are gathered into bunches in colourways.

Hydrangeas

For many cultures red is both death and life —
a beautiful and terrible paradox... red is
anger, it is fire, it is the stormy feelings
of the heart, it is the god of war,
and it is power.

Victoria Finlay, 'Colour'

The lucky staff of a major multinational bank are to have a Christmas party in a marquee at Bennelong Point, facing the Sydney Opera House with the magnificent Sydney Harbour Bridge in the background. We are asked to create a special installation in the very large open space.

The focus in the marquee is a collection of hanging baskets with peonies and trailing passionfruit vines, giving an oriental feel. The baskets are hung at different heights, so that almost the entire space between ceiling and floor is filled. Covering the ceiling, to conceal the marquee, are open paper parasols, red and white Chinese lanterns, and cane

birdcages. The parasols deflect the heat well and create a lovely waxy scent in the summer evening. Curling coils of incense join the mix to add to the suggestion of a Shanghai evening party.

Throughout the installation we hang long, trailing red ribbons, which flutter in the gentle breeze. It isn't easy to get the effect right, and it takes us a few attempts to realise just how much ribbon is required. We cut it at various lengths so that it doesn't look too contrived.

As evening falls, the darkness outside and the shimmering light on the harbour bring out the beauty of the installation.

Paradise Found

Cocoa Island is a very small, privately owned coral atoll in the Maldives, with the resort built on the sand and individual apartments built out into the Indian Ocean. A picture-perfect tropical island paradise set in an aqua-coloured sea, it's a tranquil haven for wildlife; the coral reefs around the island are home to many species of rare, colourful fish and sea animals. It's only accessible by boat so all supplies are brought in this way – we arrive by speed boat.

We're here for a wedding that will take place just outside a pavilion at the main resort. We have gatherings on the sand under the palm trees to work on the garlands, which are to be hung from the very high ceiling and around the building's central supports. The garlands consist of threaded white Singapore orchids and chrysanthemums in green and white, all ordered from China. The client has asked us to include mangrove flowers and they are brought by boat from the neighbouring island, Kandooma.

The ceremony is to be held outside, just under a cantilevered roof. We are creating an arch attached to the building. For the arch, we are using a lot of greenery, including palm leaves and monstera leaf bunches spilling out on to the roof, with blossom and threaded leis to unite the two areas, along with some green hydrangea and magnolia, all hanging inside and draped loosely out, gently blowing in the sea breeze. We are using lengths of very fine hessian fabric laid in a strip along the sand as a bridal path, decorated with chrysanthemum petals.

The couple are quiet and gentle. The bride is wearing an Akira Isogawa full-length dress with fine pleating – very simple and elegant – and carries three stems of phalaenopsis orchids tied with a taupe-coloured ribbon.

The reception dinner will be held under the stars. Green and white is the colour combination on the tables. Casual clothes, bare feet and relaxed is the order of the day, everyone walking on the flat white sand.

ORCHID FEAST

A request comes in to supply orchids for a benefit for the Children's Hospital in Sydney, so we immediately call our specialist orchid grower, Gowan, as she has never disappointed us; her passion and attention to detail are impossible to compare. Most of the orchid specimens for this charity event are graciously loaned and a few extra cut orchids have even been placed amongst the plants. Having these prized specimens transported directly from the farm to our client's doorstep helps reduce the potential for damage en route.

On arrival, three of us carry up what seems to be a forest of orchids. We set up in the kitchen with bags of moss and leather thonging, repositioning the plants in glamorous containers sourced from France and the client's own collection. We place white orchids under a traditional portrait; when we are finished, the centre table bulges with opulence and elegance.

There are whispers that Elle Macpherson will be at the event. Elle is the global ambassador for this foundation, helping raise money for the children's hospitals and paediatric research. Her appearance causes a huge stir and, as a result, we have people flocking to the shop to try to order a repeat of what we have created.

Gowan has been growing orchids for around fourteen years, and I've worked with her for about twelve. Orchid-growing started as a hobby for her and grew into a business. She is entirely self-taught — she started collecting orchids she liked because she'd enjoyed the ones in her wedding bouquet, and soon realised there was a market for different and unusual orchids. The number of orchids that are commercially viable are just the tip of the iceberg — there are over 30 000 species of orchid in the world.

saskia

Orchids

The glasshouse where Gowan grows her orchids. Some orchids require a cooler environment, but these like warmth. 'You have to create the right conditions for a plant,' she says. 'You can't buy a plant and just expect it to adapt to your conditions.'

Over the years Gowan and I have admired each other's determination and drive. The relationship is based on deep respect and a shared love of the unusual. She has never disappointed us; her passion and attention to detail are impossible to compare. Going to Gowan's is an inspiration.

Rather than green fingers, what you really need is 'green eyes', says Gowan. 'Plants will give you an indication of when they're not happy.' She's vigilant about her orchids and treats each one as carefully as a newborn.

The Blush of Youth

Never underestimate the rose; tomes have been written about its unfailing beauty. For this birthday celebration, the directive is to use pink roses, to 'emulate youth'. They will provide fragrance, colour and form; their quality and availability are always reliable in their season. Large quantities of greenery are also needed to offset the pink: we choose anthurium leaves (in larger arrangements), pilea, alocasia and emerald duke leaves as their greens are similar, creating a shadow to provide depth and contrast.

Hundreds and hundreds of pre-ordered bunches of roses arrive at our hired workspace in a neighbouring suburb: soft pink, dark and pale pink, pink tinged with a dark pink edge, orangey pink, magenta. Smooth and frilled petals are combined in a mix of flowers in bud form, semi-open and fully blown with curled outer edge petals. Painting with roses!

To fill the space above a credenza we build a structure from a thick polystyrene sheet, with two metal legs inserted to anchor it to the cabinet surface. We attach floral foam, then flowers and leaves to the polystyrene with wooden skewers, a technique I learned while working in Thailand.

Limes are used to provide another dimension and texture. When cut in half, they add wheels of pale green and a wonderful, summer-fresh fragrance. Each lime is placed on a tray and we push wooden skewers into their navels. We add them, whole or cut in half, in groups between the dark green alocasia leaves, creating a pod effect nestled into the greenery. The bundles of roses have a full, sensual look, accentuated by the round limes.

We also create an installation with the same materials that begins against the ceiling and winds its way around a pillar towards the ground. Above the bar area, at the entrance to the house, our large arrangement is hoisted up and suspended from a rail.

The party, a sit-down dinner for over 200 people, will be held in a marquee adjacent to the house. The table centrepieces comprise small alocasia leaves, peonies, some very dark red/black roses, and limes. Low square vases hold different colour combinations of roses. Eggshell-pink, white, aubergine and forest green gives a fresh, soft and delicious look, with an added ruby-red peony. I love this combination.

Fragrant Falling

I have been involved with the French company Sisley as an ambassador for the past five years, and provide flowers for their events. This time, our work with them takes us to the Art Gallery of New South Wales for the launch of a new range of fragrances. Our inspiration for the flowers comes from the colour combinations used on the packaging.

A grand entrance arrangement in a large ornate urn is filled with a tumbling, romantic, vibrant combination featuring red roses, delphiniums, orchids, passionfruit vines and silk tassel bush, forming a palette of bright red, powder blue, yellow and shades of green. Two other large arrangements on pedestals flank the second entrance, beyond which the fragrances are displayed in three sections. It's an intense, strong range of colour, picked out fresh from the morning market.

Moving into the exhibition area, we arrange the circular space into three segments, one for each fragrance, so guests can walk around the edge and experience each area independently. Each space has its own colour-themed garland threaded and pinned on to the wall behind the fragrance display: red with a hint of green; yellow and white; and purple, blue and mauve. The garlands' long trails of colour forming curved lines down each wall transform the space into a vibrant setting for this fragrance launch.

eau
de Sisley

Sweet
Avalanche

This is one of the most stressful but spectacular jobs we've ever done. It's for *Marie Claire* magazine, and is to be a grand dinner held at the Royal Hall of Industries in Sydney's former showgrounds. A huge circular table will be constructed, above which a monumental chandelier will be hung, with models suspended from it at different heights.

The table is to be adorned with numerous round glass bowls holding perfect spheres of roses. Approval on the quantity and type of rose (2000 'Sweet Avalanches') required comes through at 5 p.m. on a Thursday, a week before the event, but with Easter in between the flower market will be closed, so I have to call and text every 'Sweet Avalanche' rose grower from Gosford to Melbourne. Being persistent and polite helps, but if the roses aren't planted they're hard to produce! Our growers are incredibly

helpful and everybody takes up the challenge – one puts me in touch with the right source, so on Tuesday we are sending couriers left, right and centre to gather our bunches and bring them in to open them up for the big night. We even have extra flowers couriered direct from growers to our studio on the day of the event. The studio is filled with pink roses for three days – we could sell them ten times over.

My colleague Hannah is the straussing queen. On Thursday morning we count out all the bunches and start straussing like crazy – sixty stems per vase are whirled and twirled into the perfect rose dome.

Whilst putting together the hydrangea ball in the urn under the chandelier, I suddenly realise how ambitious this concept is: on the night, the models perched on the chandelier are breathtaking.

Hannah is our straussing queen! A bunch of roses — sixty in each bundle here — is twirled and tied into a perfect dome.

Strapping
Macrocarpa

A spring and summer fashion parade for buyers is taking place in the Hall of Industries in Sydney's old showgrounds. We collaborate with an events team for this job; we have eight meetings with the client in their office before settling on a final design which is completely different to the original concept.

We use the same raw materials for three arrangements in the entry hall and an extremely large sculptural piece inside the main hall, all standing above tall white plinths. Deciding to use Australian natives only, and just two colours, I select long branches of macrocarpa gum. A large sheet of dog-fencing wire is tethered to the wall, to which we attach the long, silvery branches of macrocarpa with strong cable ties. We need a mobile cherry picker to do this. Through this we interlace masses of tiny Cootamundra wattle – round yellow balls of fluff – making a yellow zigzag through the silver. To the wattle we add banksias and youngianas.

Australian natives have such a particular look that means they work best in sculptural arrangements; they are not sentimental. Many native flowers are very small – they are botanical wonders, with a sort of prehistoric quality; strange and intellectually interesting, quite aloof.

By the Willow, in the Rain, in the Evening

A Moreton Bay fig provided a spooky backdrop.

The chairs had to be kept covered in plastic to keep the rain off, giving them a ghostly look.

The work we do is not always about conventional beauty; sometimes it's about creating a mood, such as the dark and decadent theme for this job. Part of Sydney Fashion Week, it is taking place in the garden of a private eastern suburbs home. We arrive for a site inspection only days before the event, which is not unusual for Fashion Week participants; they are renowned for working well under pressure.

It is to be a very large sit-down dinner for ninety people, set along a massive long table on a path leading to the house. The weather is inclement and ominous. We try to dodge the downpours as we move things into position. My team is soaked and shivering and there are no hot beverages in sight.

There is a magnificent, 100-year-old Moreton Bay fig tree at the water's edge; it is dark, dense and mysterious and at twilight certainly gives the impression that creatures of the night could be lurking! Ladders lean against the convoluted trunk, and long swings are hung from its branches. Fifteen models like alluring gazelles float above the incoming tide, toes trailing the water, feet encased in very high platform boots which extend to the top of the thigh, like leggings!

At 5 p.m. I notice our lighting man setting up a workspace in the garage. He is creating a look of the Amazon; the row of trees lining the drive will look amazing lit from behind.

Trucks arrive with massive canvas umbrellas to fend off the storm and protect the tables and chairs. Paint is dripping off the black chairs on to our hands and clothes. Our team begin to install, carrying branches, rare plants, test tube vases, orchids, leaves, candles, moss, terrariums, black roses, driftwood and work tools up and down the steep driveway. To add to the pressure, we need to start work on another fashion show at 3.30 a.m. the next day. A coffee run lifts our spirits and so do a few laughs. However, due to the rain we can't really place anything until about 6.30 p.m., and the dinner starts at 8 p.m.

Umbrellas are wedged between tables and covered with plastic, as are the chairs, to prevent any more paint coming off. Suddenly the rain slows down; hair and make-up artists and models arrive and excitement is breaking through the earlier nervousness.

Now we need to create the look on the dining table between crockery and cutlery, so we shift and fumble along the edge of the table with a lot of 'Excuse me', 'Excuse me' to waiters and catering staff, placing table decorations that are intriguing, including framed insects such as scorpions, stick insects, gnarly-looking beetles, large dusty moths and Ulysses butterflies. We use many test tube and specimen vases to lend a scientific, experimental look, filling them with unusual orchids and delicate leaves. A lot of Dutchman's pipe flowers with their trailing vines and leaves are used; these are shortlived and hard to find, oval-shaped with a dark brown centre, speckled green and cream. They've been grown to perfection specifically for this job, and picked this morning by a good friend of my mother's. There are also Venus flytraps and pitcher plants lit by glass lamps and candle, and as many black roses as possible.

The recorded sound of birds and insects contribute to the extraordinary ambience. If only we had 'the singing orchids' from J G Ballard's story 'Prima Belladonna' that couldn't bear to hear the nightclub chanteuse sing, or a few of his 'mutating plants'. A row of tall fir trees behind the table are lit in such a way that they look like a rock face.

The decorated entryway is extremely wet, though the atmosphere is strange and enticing. I totter along a stone wall to place storm lanterns, anticipating departing guests getting lost in the greenery or the stormy weather. At times like this I'm reminded of my mother, a ballet dancer, saying, 'A few more pliés', 'A few more pliés'. That sort of discipline comes into play when you have to keep going until you've perfected the work and made it look really effortless.

Our
Lady of the
Camellias

Johanna's wedding is being held under a large Moreton Bay fig on the lawn outside the Palm House at the Royal Botanic Gardens in Sydney. Johanna is a longstanding member of the Grandiflora team, so we have no trouble interpreting her floral ideas. She has always had the romantic image of being married surrounded by camellias and especially loves cut cyclamen flowers. The Palm House has an innate charm and it's situated in the middle of green lawns on to which the guests can wander.

We arrive as a team in two vans escorted by the garden ranger. All hands are on deck – even husbands and children are lassoed into helping, scrambling up ladders and passing sundries and flowers to each other. Our courier Greg sets up the entire bar single-handedly. Such camaraderie.

The roof and ceiling are gently pitched, with fine-looking wooden rafters. For this event we create an intimate atmosphere by decorating the ceiling with masses of greenery to fill the space above the long central table, later to be laden with a breakfast feast for the guests.

As Mrs Beeton might have said, 'First find your camellia trees.'

A grower supplies thick green camellia foliage and large, very long branches that fill an entire van, together with beautiful, delicate pink 'Lady Loch' camellia flowers. Single white sasanqua and 'Lovelight' blooms have been selected from a specialised camellia nursery north-west of Sydney. An arch crowning the front door is made with ornamental fig, growing figs and camellias, and is fixed on to the entrance with G-clamps.

We create an arch at the next entrance by placing antique ladders on either side of the room. Tall camellia branches, ordered two months previously, are tied on with strong rope, with five branches in each bundle to create good density and make them very secure. More branches are arched over the top, and the entire structure is decorated with clusters of roses.

We place a large arrangement between the two arches at the door in an exotic, ornate-footed silver container. Heavy-headed 'Weber's Parrot' tulips combine with striped and coloured camellias. Along the centre table we place cyclamen along with camellias in specimen vases. The

cake is low and pink with a couple of very full white camellias on top to match the single camellia worn by Johanna in her hair.

In the ceremony area on the lawn, under the protective arm of the Moreton Bay fig, we drape garlands made from trailing camellia branches with small bunches of cymbidium orchids and ornamental figs worked in to create a luscious look. The couple marry under this floral bough.

On the signing table sits an intricate antique vase of wire-bound test tubes whose small apertures make the perfect vehicle for holding single stems of 'Weber's Parrot' tulips and camellias. We make paper cones of rose petals to be scattered instead of confetti and place them on each chair. The scattered petals look soft and beautiful at the completion of the ceremony, a dappled carpet. Everyone wants to take a picture.

Candles are lit along with warming braziers on the lawn, as it's a chilly winter morning – the gentle smoke adding to the subtle romantic mood. A barista makes coffees to warm the hands, hearts and bodies of the congregation. Unusually, we stay on to enjoy the day as a group, and it makes our day to relax and settle into the mood of the morning.

Camellias are a very delicate flower and have to be picked as close to the time they're needed as possible if you want them to look their best, preferably on the day. This means lots of pressure - there have been plenty of times when I've been driving out to collect them and thought, 'This is insane.' But it's always worth it in the end.

Camellias are so elegant and simple — my favourite is 'Lovelight', but all of them take my breath away.

Lovelight

These are specimen camellias — the very best examples of the camellias available. You can't just buy these flowers at the market, so I really appreciate the support the grower gives me in supplying them so perfectly unmarked.

The shredded paper is to protect the flowers.

'Butlune 'N Boms' CAMELLION x WILLIANSII

Camellias

Radiant Sister of the Day

Radiant sister of the day
awake! arise! and come away!
To the wild woods and the plains
and the pools where winter rains
image all their roof of leaves
where the pine its garland
of sapless green and ivy dun weaves
round stems that never kiss the sun.
Percy Bysshe Shelley, 'The Invitation'

One afternoon, we get a call from the art director Mark Vassallo. We've worked with him before and have always enjoyed his creativity, and the way he provokes our loose, untamed edges. Can we provide an arrangement for a shoot early the next morning? The concept is 'A fashion fairytale; a whimsical white Christmas', and the directive is to look contemporary, bleached and not too organised. Yes, we can! We have two hours to conceive, plan and create the concept before our studio shuts at 6 p.m., after which we'll need to take all the raw elements with us and work onsite.

We build a structure of gum branches and flowers, selecting twisted willow, blossom, fern, rice flowers, and lichen-covered sticks, securing it all with sandbags on the floor. All things strong go first, then we decorate them with bundles and bunches of smaller, more delicate material, adding and taking away, re-arranging, lengthening, creating more height and loosening up dense areas to look papery and see-through.

After we settle in, there seems to be a lot of waiting but luckily we are in a very glamorous studio with a beautiful array of fruit and breakfast. The place is quite different to what we are used to, but we need to be on set to keep an eye on our structure, and in case Mark needs us to change anything. The model is the insanely beautiful Miranda Kerr. The result is images that are feathery, wispy and surreal.

The Scarlet Pimpernel

Supper had been extremely gay.
All those present declared that
never had Lady Blakeney been
more adorable, nor... Sir Percy
more amusing.

Baroness Orczy,
'The Scarlet Pimpernel'

We have an appointment to meet at The Country Trader to select a site and props for a red-themed private dinner. The setting is to be at our discretion – we have no restrictions. An open brief! How fantastic. The Country Trader is an incredible place to garner ideas: a cavernous warren of rooms, full of precious relics and antiques, all displayed with an artist's eye. We take inspiration from there, and from *The Scarlet Pimpernel*, a novel set in revolutionary France – an atmosphere of intrigue, danger and excitement.

Against a backdrop based on the fifteenth-century *Lady and the Unicorn* series of tapestries from the Cluny Museum in Paris, we choose a round table with a seventeenth-century French limestone Corinthian capital base. Remnants of the central floral base with classical acanthus scrolls join a collar, now inverted on a square plinth, to support a glass top. A selection of 1930s-style Pauchard chairs, painted fire-engine red,

and others with dramatic high backs, add to the theatrical scale.

We suspend two large antique elk and deer horn chandeliers with red lamp shades above the table, decorated with ivy and mixed fruticosa garlands with 'Henri Matisse' roses, red carnations and a very petite black gerbera. The installation hangs dramatically low, just clearing the guests' heads.

We decide it would be more innovative not to have a table centrepiece, but instead to place foliage of many green shades under the glass so our guests can enjoy looking down at the flowers below. Igniting candles at foot level gives us an edge. Is it safe? We test it out ourselves – yes! The base of the table is far enough away from the guests' feet and we make sure the foliage and flowers are kept away from the flame.

A daring and beautifully enchanting, burlesque mood. I'm picturing cigars and elegantly dressed women; it's all taking shape.

Foraging Tussy-Mussy

The father of the bride for this wedding, to be held on the family property, hopes that one day this will be the largest landscaped garden in the southern hemisphere; a staff of five full-time gardeners work here and the plan is to eventually have a moss garden; specific areas for cactus, herbs, lavender, roses, stone and citrus fruit; and a Chinese garden, kitchen garden and cut-flower garden. Our directive for this wedding is 'home-grown, selected and hand-picked from the garden, and lovingly placed in the table centres'. We are generously assigned a team of 'pickers' from the garden staff, as all the foliage and greenery will be from the property. We intend a 'tussy-mussy' look – a Victorian posy of an eclectic mixture of elements – but on a really grand scale; like a Dutch Master's floral still life.

Driving toward the property in Oberon in the Blue Mountains near Sydney, one is struck by the landscape: lush rolling green pastures, and magnificent eucalyptus trees and conifers flanking the road.

The entrance to the property is marked by mounds of lavender. We're surrounded by clipped green grass, a great canvas for colourful flowers. We bring with us a quantity of specialty floral specimens from the flower market in Sydney, as well as many dahlias from our grower, Barry.

A family chapel has been built over the past five months especially for this event; the interior is pared back and simple, featuring a dry stone wall, wall lamps, metal girders and a stunning view of the red earth sprinkled with bright green shrubbery. There is an arch behind the altar that we decorate with trailing greenery and white/yellow roses with a small number of bunched blue hydrangeas. The bride loves blue flowers. For her bouquet we wire individual blue delphinium flowers into a round shape, with clusters of small blue hydrangeas between.

The celebration is held in a marquee. Armando Percuoco from Sydney's Buon Ricordo and his team come to take care of the wedding feast. We work in the cool of the pump room attached to the main house, creating haphazard, eclectic, baroque, full-on arrangements under each chandelier, aiming to intrigue the guests. There are many large, heavy crystal vases containing arrangements along the length of two long tables, seating two hundred people altogether, using roses, orchids, dahlias, tulips, persimmons, fennel, geranium, celosia, crab apple, rosemary, touches of blue hydrangea and foliage in varying shades and tones of green, all highlighted with a peppering of elements from the cutting garden.

Our dahlia grower Barry is a rock 'n' roll musician who used to be a postman; he now grows dahlias simply because he loves them. I met him through a friend of a friend at a trivia night for my daughter's school - she called across the tables to me, 'You just have to see these amazing dahlias!' I wasn't convinced at first - some people look down on dahlias and think they are a bit 'common' so I wasn't sure I'd be able to sell them - but when I saw these I was blown away. They are glorious, and so huge! Barry drives them to us himself and they always go straight into our window.

The dahlias that Barry is holding are called 'Winkie Hooper'. We love saying it in the shop!

Dahlias

A new strain comes out every year as the bees cross-pollinate them naturally. I always look forward to seeing what they will do next.

Dahlias have a fairly short season - just six to eight weeks in summer - so we have to make the most of them while we can.

ROSES EN POINTE

Vive, sensible, peu coquette
suivons la gloire et les plaisirs.
C'est a la fois la violette
la rose amante du zephyr
elle s'emporte, elle s'apaise
elle pleure et sourit tour a tour.

(Lively, sensitive, a little flirtatious,
let's follow glory and pleasure.
She's the violet,
she's the rose caressed by the breeze,
she flares up, she calms down,
she smiles and weeps in turn.)

Edgar Degas

To my family and me, the National Gallery of Australia in Canberra is a hallowed Mecca, so to be asked to do the benefactors' dinner whilst the Degas exhibition is showing has great allure! The day before the event, we are signed in to the gallery as guests and given an induction on safety issues, the spaces we'll work in and the logistics of the job. A lot of loading of trolleys and pushing them up to our workspace is done so that all is ready for the next day.

I need two vans and two buyers, shopping on the spot and collecting flowers we have pre-ordered. We collect quantities of imported pink roses as well as locally grown ones – called, funnily enough, 'Henri Matisse'. Leo Schofield has described these as 'splashed with bold brushstrokes of raspberry and white'. We are using these stripy pink roses in great quantities. Trailing conifer (found one day at a grower's property whilst we were being taken on a tractor tour) is used to cover the pots containing very long-stemmed roses and dahlias.

Colours match Degas' paintings, delicate and soft with black where possible – a sort of French look. Tall specimen vases adorn the tables, holding deep pink roses graduating into tones of pale pink, reminiscent of the flowers in Restaurant Georges, at the top of the Pompidou Centre in Paris.

We aren't able to set up in the area where the dinner will take place because working there with glass and water is not allowed. Conservation is also concerned about any insects that might damage the artworks. We give a firm guarantee that all our raw material is insect-free, having used a pesticide recommended by the gallery.

We begin after 5 p.m. on Friday under the watchful eye of security – we are now the only people in the gallery. By 9 a.m. the next day there is already a queue at the front door. Our strategy is to work hard for the first half of the day so we'll have time to consider and rearrange if necessary towards the end of the job.

I have a trolley to work on for the large arrangement, making it easier to deal with the three-dimensional aspect, as I can spin it around and alternately add dahlias and the cascading conifer greenery to disguise the container. The arrangement becomes trailing and low, rather than tall and wide; more poetic and not so densely structured. This ties in beautifully with the enormous image of a Degas painting behind it – it is thrilling to see this all come together.

The client suggests we might like to see the Degas exhibition. As the gallery is closed, it is a private viewing with just the three of us. It is such a privilege to see the paintings at our leisure, unhurried. Knowing that scores of people have bustled through just before us, we know that we are privileged.

We pack ourselves into the van and drive back to Sydney, arriving at 2 a.m. to get ready to pack up for another floral adventure.

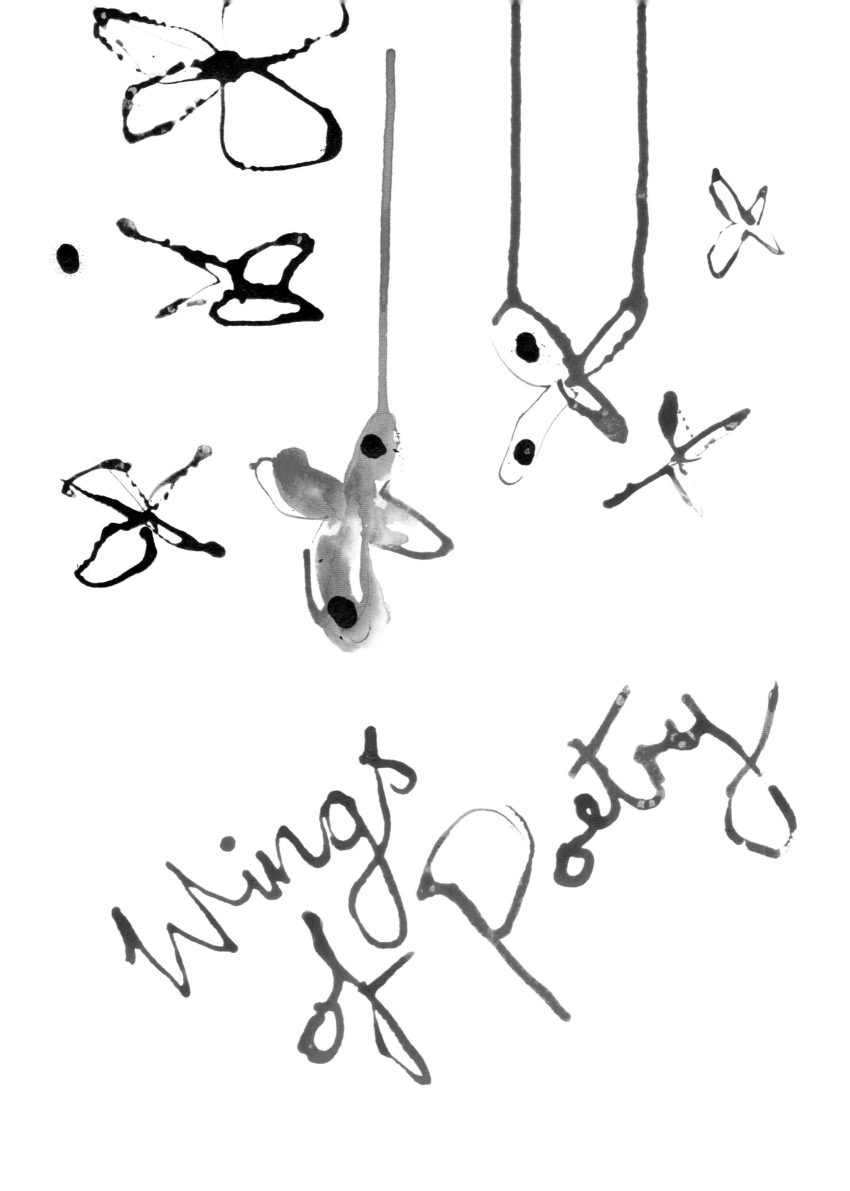

A jewellery company is launching a couture line at Guillaume at Bennelong restaurant at the Sydney Opera House at a sit-down dinner for 150 people. The secret special guest is Blondie, who will entertain the guests with a set from a stage right in the middle of the room. The client provides a photograph for colour reference, and the brief is 'underwater dark depths of colour, up into fresh air – dark green, blue, magenta, pink to white, strange shapes and forms'.

We collaborate with Sydney artist Nell to create a huge mobile suspended from the ceiling within the atrium of the restaurant. It hangs in parallel lines at different lengths from the roof and consists of many components threaded onto fishing line. Extra-large sequins grade down to very small, glinting and sparkling with natural skeleton leaves in between. Tulle, chiffon and thin nylon fabric, some of it covered in chainmail, is cut into simple shapes. They vary in lengths, all shimmering and sparkling, many nuances and textures.

Sprinkled generously between all of this are feather butterflies. They settle on the wheatgrass and amongst the vegetation.

Glass vases of vastly differing widths and heights are placed along the tables with coloured candles in each, also different heights and widths. Crimson phalaenopsis orchid heads are placed in clusters around the base of these, providing flecks and flashes of mysterious colour.

We have grown trays of wheatgrass to line the stair rails and the entrance, and planter boxes are also filled with extra-large-leaf monstera, fiddler fig, cardamom and ginger leaves, maidenhair fern in concealed pots to fill areas to give a rainforest look, and huge bamboo for height.

Blondie, clad completely in black, rehearses while we set up, and the amplification is so powerful we think Bennelong will take off. It is the most fantastic party of the year.

TRAILING
Creeping
GROWING

Club 21 is a Singapore-based global luxury retail company with department stores in Singapore, Bangkok and Indonesia, showcasing Alexander McQueen, Lanvin, Balenciaga, Martin Margiela, Dries Van Noten and also our own Akira Isogawa.

When I mention working in Singapore, my friends think it sounds exotic and exciting, and it is, but the humidity has to be accounted for; we are unused to working in such heat. Spreading the workload over many people is very helpful. It can be easy to feel overwhelmed and daunted by a job of this size as it gains momentum.

The event is a spring fashion launch, and the trusty Club 21 team is here, eager to help us wrangle and manoeuvre, shift and shape the flowers. Our blooms open faster in the more humid environment so it is important to factor this in. We have eight people to help us 'process' the flowers; this means undoing strapped and stapled boxes, peeling away paper and/ or synthetic cushions for the blooms, re-cutting the stems and placing them quickly into buckets of water. We need people lifting and carrying buckets of water, vases, props, flowers, drop sheets, ladders, secateurs, cable ties and plants. We have quite a few areas to decorate, working mainly in colour blocks, with combinations like blues and purples through to aubergine for 'cool'; tomato, burnt orange, pinks and red for 'warm'; and whites and creams for balance.

At the store's entrance we set up an extravagant collection of vases. We position each of the vessels on a massive wooden table, creating a composition of different textures, colours, heights and shapes. Then, in direct reference to the illustrated invitation, we fill each one with a profusion of 'garden' flowers, meaning flowers chosen for their unique individual beauty and matched with other elements in a way that creates rhythm and tone and adds to the visual sum of their collective appeal. Above all, it means flowers that are not overly manicured, and are selected and composed in an unhurried manner.

For many weeks before we embark on a project such as this we email back and forth, developing relationships with growers and scanning the market from a distance. Working in Singapore brings into focus the amazing quality and choice of the raw materials available at Sydney's flower markets. In Singapore, we buy peonies from Israel, tulips from Holland, hydrangeas from Kenya, roses from China, hoya and tuberoses from Malaysia – only the orchids are from local Singapore markets. Usually we prefer to buy local, to lessen our 'footprint' and support the local community and economy.

The team in Singapore has a lot of organising to do for this project and they do it with verve! There are tools to be gathered, plant roots to be washed, and the hoya takes on a life of its own: its one hundred-plus plants need to be extracted from their pots and their roots washed before being placed on the screen structures to show off the beauty of their leaves and the creeping, growing vine that cascades and drapes. These plants are selected for their longevity as they are hardy and only need to be sprayed daily to stay alive for days.

We cut down the tuberoses to place in low circular vases, twenty bunches in each – there is great movement in all the tips and buds. We use a mountain of moss to cover the plastic pots and to line the insides of the glass vases. An incredible jasmine tree is placed in an exquisite glass vase designed in South Africa. We use live trees for height and vigour, placing them amongst vases of cut arranged blooms – this makes the installation feel less predictable.

Eddy, our Singapore contact, is busily adding lukewarm water to the roses to open them up as they have arrived very tight. He is going back to the market in the morning to find beautiful Japanese Hill moss (impossible to find in Australia) to cover the outsides of the pots we are placing on the eclectic main table.

The windows that span the vast distance between the Four Seasons Hotel and the Hilton Hotel are adorned with beautiful botanical illustrations of old-fashioned flowers – this event is in every way a work of art. The flowers we choose are in keeping with these illustrations and the exquisite invitation. True to this decadent point of departure we thread copious amounts of fresh flowers through the framework of purpose-built screens, each commanding an enormous space. We allocate the screens two colour combinations: blue, purple and lime-green; and burgundy, gold and pink.

Our team at Grandiflora has such a sympathetic communication system – we laugh about the fact that when we are on location working we don't need spoken instructions; often it's just a grunt, or an expression on someone's face, that might send a co-worker running to collect more jasmine or extra florist wire. So when I make a 'mock-up' of an event for my team, they go off and create it with their own interpretive flair, which is critical to articulating the Grandiflora look – all parts make a whole.

By contrast, the team in Singapore is unfailingly accurate in interpreting my work, so we need to work hard to 'loosen up'. After giving what, in retrospect, I realise was not enough instruction (or was it too much?), I leave them to it. When I return they have impressively threaded flowers through a large portion of the screens. But the colours are too mixed and it all has to be pulled down and begun again with the emphasis on colour blocking. Disappointing for them, difficult for me. But over the years I have had to learn to assert myself to ensure the success of the finished product.

The hospitality of our client in Singapore is quite phenomenal. We are treated daily to enormous banquets of the finest exotic fare that Singapore has to offer, one of our favourites being a succulent steamed white chicken dish drizzled with soy and sesame oil accompanied by the most delicious garlicky-chilli dip, all served on a bed of fragrant rice. It's seriously addictive!

I am invited to the event, as it is also a book launch and an opportunity for me to talk about Grandiflora and my work with flowers. I sign books and talk with many inspiring and interesting people. The atmosphere is buzzing and it is a treat to dress up and mingle after working.

Spice Mural

A birthday party for a client is to be held in the Art Deco hall at the Museum of Contemporary Art in Sydney. The room features marble columns, very high ceilings and high, elongated windows; our main floral decorations will serve partly to fill the gap between the table surfaces and the ceiling to create an intimacy; from a distance they become 'floral murals', a first for us.

This is a very organised job with a lot of advance planning needed as there are many technical aspects. A long lead time is unusual for us, and as a result the final placing of flowers and the positioning of the structure is relatively smooth. A luscious, subtropical Indian look evolves and we prepare many garlands in our studio. Colour combinations are decided before ordering from the growers, and the final placing is all done onsite.

For the 'big ceiling treatment', two structures are made from wooden planks, to be hoisted up into position once they are completed. When the arrangements are complete, it's time to hoist the structures into position. They rise in the air, two Grandiflorettes on one end and two men on the other carefully working the pulleys. It's such a huge weight to lift and we have to make sure all the chains are pulled at the same speed – there is an engineer on hand telling us to slow down or pull more on one side than another. We calculate how much weight the structures will take so we know how much foliage and flowers to suspend. The structure alone with all the water-soaked oasis is heavy without any decoration, so we have to maintain a fine balance.

Once the structures are secure, we continue to work on them, a very daunting experience. We subsequently refer to this time as 'The Hoist'. Suspended three metres off the ground, with the lighting picking out specific areas of colour, the structures shimmer, giving a lot of life to the room.

There are no table arrangements, only crockery, glasses and beautiful imported tapered candles of great length.

We clothe the structures in dried lotus leaves sprayed bronze in fan-like shapes. To these we add sprays of saffron dancing lady orchids in bundles, bixa, deep red cymbidium orchids, kale of many colours, amber-coloured roses, clusters of colour-perfect navel oranges and sweet william (which we spray appropriate colours, as it's such a good laster and shape). All these combine to evoke a spectacular kaleidoscopic look of India, a variety of visual experience inspired by vegetation from palm-fringed coasts to snow-capped mountains, subtle hints of perfume, and the vivid, magical mixing of colour. The food also provides colour, aromatically spiced with yellow saffron, red-hot chilli and paprika.

a Rose is a Rose is a Rose

You love the roses—so do I. I wish
The sky would rain down roses, as they rain
From off the shaken bush. Why will it not?
Then all the valley would be pink and white
And soft to tread on. They would fall as light
As feathers, smelling sweet; and it would be
Like sleeping and like waking, all at once!

George Eliot, 'Roses'

Roses certainly speak for themselves, and they speak volumes in this very feminine floral concept. It's a lavish seventy-fifth birthday party and the look is 'an abundance of roses'.

Because of their thorns, roses are very labour-intensive to prepare, but they are totally worth the effort, especially the fragrant ones. Along with gardenias and camellias, they are the classic blooms representing femininity. We are lucky to have them available in such a phenomenal colour range in this country.

The event is a dinner under the stars. The stylist comes up with the fresh concept of colour-coded cushions. Each table has its own set of velvet cushions in allotted colours. On arrival, guests are given a button covered in coloured fabric so they can easily find their seats.

The roses arrive the evening before the event at 5.30 p.m. from our grower Paula's farm. We can't fit them all in to our studio, so we line them up on the footpath against the wall outside. The passing traffic is fascinated; soon there are swarms of people gathered in the street, the like of which we've never seen before. Up to twenty people at a time stand gaping, some rushing home to get their cameras to document what is going on. It generates a huge amount of interest and a lot of questions.

But at 8 p.m. a representative from the council appears and threatens to close us down. 'No working on the footpath', we are told, 'or after hours'. But there is so much to do! We move the flowers to our nearby office and keep working on what we can in the studio, with papered-up windows.

We are installing trailing flowers down the 4.5-metre-long entrance hall of the house to create a look of relaxed opulence. Copious pink and cream-coloured roses sit above peppercorn foliage to give a cascading waterfall of colour and form.

The centrepieces for the tables consist of low vases with roses, pomegranates, peppercorns and tulips, all in mauves and soft pinks. Organic beeswax tea-light candles in glass vessels create a romantic ambience.

I adore the outdoor cigar lounge area under a chandelier, which hangs from a tree. Here guests can sign the birthday book.

For another feature area, where the guests move from drinks to dining, we arrange garden roses in cut crystal urns and oversized goldfish bowls on five mirrored pedestals to maximise the look of abundance. We don't mix in any other flowers. We light sparkly tea-light candles in small glass bowls to create an intimate light source during the evening.

Finally we construct a massive floral shelf, a transparent 'floating' table, as a surreal vision against a glass wall with Sydney Harbour in the background. On the shelf are masses of pre-tied eclectic groupings of flowers. Three of us return at 10 p.m, wearing matching aprons made for the event, armed with all the equipment to assemble bunches made from these flowers for guests to take home. Plastic sheets for wet stems, tape, square-cut sheets of tracing paper and tissue, scissors, ribbon and sprayer are all at the ready for sixty gifts to be distributed at the front door as the guests depart, along with a handwritten note. This is a new concept for us, and the sight of the ribbon-wrapped bunches flanking the stairs waiting for the receiving arms of guests is breathtakingly generous.

We do lots of work with Paula, our main supplier of roses. She's been in the business all her life. She's very dedicated and is constantly updating her knowledge; she is passionate about roses and is very interested in the older and less mainstream varieties such as 'Chartreuse de Parme', 'Spirit of Peace' and 'Birmingham Post'. Paula often helps us of her own accord and works hard to make sure she knows what we need. We're always learning from each other.

When the roses are in bloom, usually from October to June, picking and packing is a seven-days-a-week job. We are extremely grateful for the extent to which her team pushes themselves.

Roses

Paula sells half-open flowers rather than tightly budded ones, leaving them on the bush until they're perfect. It's unusual for a grower to be prepared to take that kind of risk, as the flowers are more easily bruised when they're open, so they need to be handled carefully and transported in buckets.

Keeping an eye on the roses, so they're picked at the point of perfection, is time-consuming, but Paula says it's worth it.

Technicolour Dreamers

We are very honoured to be asked to collaborate in a wedding to be held in the coveted venue of the Art Gallery of New South Wales. We are to make a huge wall of colour that uses flowers to match the intensity and diversity of Kandinsky's artistic palette, hectic unexpected colour combinations, and a twist on Jeff Koons' *Puppy*. We hope to achieve this with thousands of gerberas creating a riot of colour and shape.

Kandinsky is believed to have had synaesthesia, a condition that allows a person to appreciate sounds, colours or words with two or more senses simultaneously. In his case, colours and painted marks triggered particular sounds or musical notes. Kandinsky said 'The harmony of colour and form must be based solely upon the principle of proper contact with the human soul', and his work was characterised by a feeling for colour – patterned, stippled dots and spots, wildly vibrating and interacting. An artist can suggest something of the landscape and the seasons of nature with line, density of colour and space. Other notable technicolour dreamers who had the same condition include Baudelaire, Vladimir Nabokov and David Hockney.

We need a lot of people to get things ready after the gallery doors shut at 5 p.m. and the public leave. We create the wall from crates, as the open surfaces allow us to place oasis inside. Into these we place gerberas with their strong fleshy petals of saturated colour. It is really the zing of green in between the gerberas that makes the effect pulsate. We have a very short time frame and I am determined for it to be astonishing as we have never used gerberas before.

At the entrance to the area where the wedding is to take place we arrange a cascade of maidenhair fern on long, tall, narrow plinths, with cream and white gerberas and ranunculas along the top. This creates a calm, elegant contrast to the reds and oranges, and a spectacular aisle for the bride.

CENTRE
STAGE

Cate Blanchett asks us to adorn a dinner taking place on the stage of the Sydney Theatre Company in Walsh Bay. This time it is florists setting up backstage instead of actors.

As it's a fundraiser, we've been asked to keep the concept quite simple. The table decorations are to favour pink, so we use very hot pink garden roses, offset by pilea leaves in all shades of green from very dark to the palest shimmery green. This little leaf is easy to grow from a cutting, and is a very useful addition. All encased in resin vases of varying shapes and heights from Dinosaur Designs that have a pink-and-white swirly marble effect. In the theatre foyer we use black perspex vases with wavy, irregular sides, filled with immature phalaenopsis orchids, all in the deepest pink.

We are backstage with our floral elements, soft and delicate in contrast to the cords and concrete of this cavernous work area, setting up where so many revered performers have 'gone on' from. We are creating centrepieces for the twenty rectangular tables set for dinner onstage, staging for our 'performance', using an actors' space out front on a table with white cloths, the room surrounded by black drapes.

A few weeks previously, we embarrassingly wheeled our clattering trolley rather loudly backstage while a matinee was taking place. Fortunately, tonight the only performance is this fundraising dinner, and our flowers are centre stage.

Royal Purple

Purple is the colour of royalty,
the colour of Cleopatra's sails
and of Bacchus's wine-stained
lips. It's the colour of the highest
vestments of priesthood, and
perhaps of Homer's wine-dark
sea. It is seductive and
mysterious, sacred and profane.

French luxury fashion house is hosting a dinner. They have stipulated that we use purple, and they would like two sumptuous arrangements in large boat-shaped containers on either side of the steps. There are to be no flowers on the round dining tables; deep purple cloths and a central glass crystal ball are to be the only decoration, along with beautiful Hèrmes plates.

It takes some time to get the colour right. We decide on pink lilies, 'Queen of the Night' tulips, peeled back, with figs on their branches, dark purple hydrangeas, deep crimson celosia, vanda orchids, 'Clear Water' roses, and black/purple callas. We're going for a sumptuous look, which requires a lot of flowers. Trailing and cascading amaranthus, ferns and delicate vines cover the bases and plinths. We layer the flowers with fuller areas and arrange ferns, greenery and levels of flowers in dark, rich purple tones for a mysterious, deep opulent look. The next day we have numerous phone calls to congratulate us on the extravagance of the arrangement – it really strikes a chord.

Blossom High

I do not love you as if you were salt-rose, or topaz,
or the arrow of carnations the fire shoots off.
I love you as certain dark things are to be loved,
in secret, between the shadow and the soul.

I love you as the plant that never blooms
but carries in itself the light of hidden flowers;
thanks to your love a certain solid fragrance,
risen from the earth, lives darkly in my body.

I love you without knowing how, or when, or from where.
I love you straight forwardly, without complexities or pride;
so I love you because I know no other way

than this: where I does not exist, nor you,
so close that your hand on my chest is my hand,
so close that your eyes close as I fall asleep.

Pablo Neruda, 'Sonnet XVII'

The journey from initial concept meeting to the final result is always a unique experience. No event is ever the same. We pride ourselves on our bespoke designs and close collaboration with our clients, and this often requires many meetings and lots of workshopping. My favourite part of the process is the debrief I have with my colleagues in the van when the job is completed. It's then I feel most personally challenged – we share what went well and what didn't. It's a time to reflect on lessons learnt and to feel the thrill of achievement. One of our most memorable wedding events gives us this thrill after we complete our part.

The wedding takes place at the beginning of spring in the crypt under Sydney's St Mary's Cathedral, followed by a reception at the Wharf Restaurant. In the planning stages, I meet with the bride-to-be to discuss images that she and I have collated for inspiration – pictures of garden parties at sumptuous villas in Italy, extravagant images from Paris and decadent wedding books. We sit at the end of the Grandiflora workbench and pull together container samples and pictures of flowers that will be in season at the time of the wedding.

We meet at both the restaurant and the crypt so I can assess the size of the arrangements required and work out how and when I will get them in, as well as the lighting, the finishes on the floors and walls and the overall mood of the venue, all of which will help determine what we select. We decide that abundant spring blossom is to be the theme in both the crypt and the restaurant.

We find the right blossom in the Blue Mountains to the west of Sydney, and place orders months in advance. The grower keeps a few trees tagged especially for us. These have long limbs, which we'll need to achieve an arch shape at the altar, constructed by using tall tapered heavy glass vases and leaning the branches towards each other. In total, we need three van-loads of blossom to decorate both the crypt and the restaurant. In addition to the blossom arch, we install a magnificent explosion of blossom and jasmine near the entrance to the crypt the night before the wedding. The scent on the day is wonderfully romantic.

For the reception, the client has asked me to decorate the vast ceiling of the restaurant. There will be five generous bunches of blossom branches tumbling down from on high. We'll need very tall ladders; you'd usually use a cherry-picker for this sort of project but none are available on the day. In the end many extra (and very muscular) hands and arms are needed to transport the blossom branches to the site and then lever them into position.

Each of the table arrangements are slightly different. It is a very sophisticated and feminine concept, and flowers of graded heights are allowed to drape over the edges of the vases. We use a variety of glass vases – etched, cut crystal, goldfish bowls and other eclectic containers. Blooms include pieris, anemones in nude colours with a slight blush of pink, roses in antique tones, lily of the valley, hellebores, sweetpeas, camellias and cyclamen. There are no flowers on the central table except for the delightfully understated wedding cake, decorated only with ranunculas. Candles, in containers of various heights, surround and seem to protect it.

The day of the wedding is the first, superb day of spring. The sun is beaming down and I know the bride will be happy; she could not have wished for a more beautiful day. However, we find we have several unexpected hurdles to overcome.

At 7 a.m. we bolt from the flower markets to the restaurant with laden vans to set up. Everything has to be prepared before their regular lunch service. We arrive at 8 a.m. to find the intercom isn't working to get the boom gate up, so I have to perform a high-speed sprint down the length of the wharf to encourage the restaurant to let us in. As we are beginning to negotiate the enormous bundles of blossom branches into the heights of the ceiling, a large man appears, furious at the trail of blossom we have left behind whilst unloading in the car park, and threatens to sue us for thousands of dollars. We have never swept so fast.

After suspending the blossoms at the restaurant, it's time to install the arrangements in the crypt and add extra jasmine. By now it's 11 a.m. and we are trying to pin down a very shy sacristan to work out when he can open the crypt for us. And as if time isn't already against me, I drop the key to the crypt down the grate at the front door, and have to crawl on my stomach and reach into the drain to retrieve it – just an hour or two before the bride is to arrive.

At 3 p.m. we are able to get back to the restaurant to start our centrepieces. It has all come together and it is such a thrill when we see the bride and groom having a magnificent time at the reception. The bride looks divine in her Collette Dinnigan vintage dress and the size of her bouquet is perfect. The groom catches sight of us, sweeps up a glass of champagne, raises it to us and calls out how much he loved the flowers at the crypt. Wow, what a man! And what a clever bride to be marrying a flower lover.

We use sailing rope to bind huge bundles of spring blossom into natural chandeliers, then hoist them over the rafters.

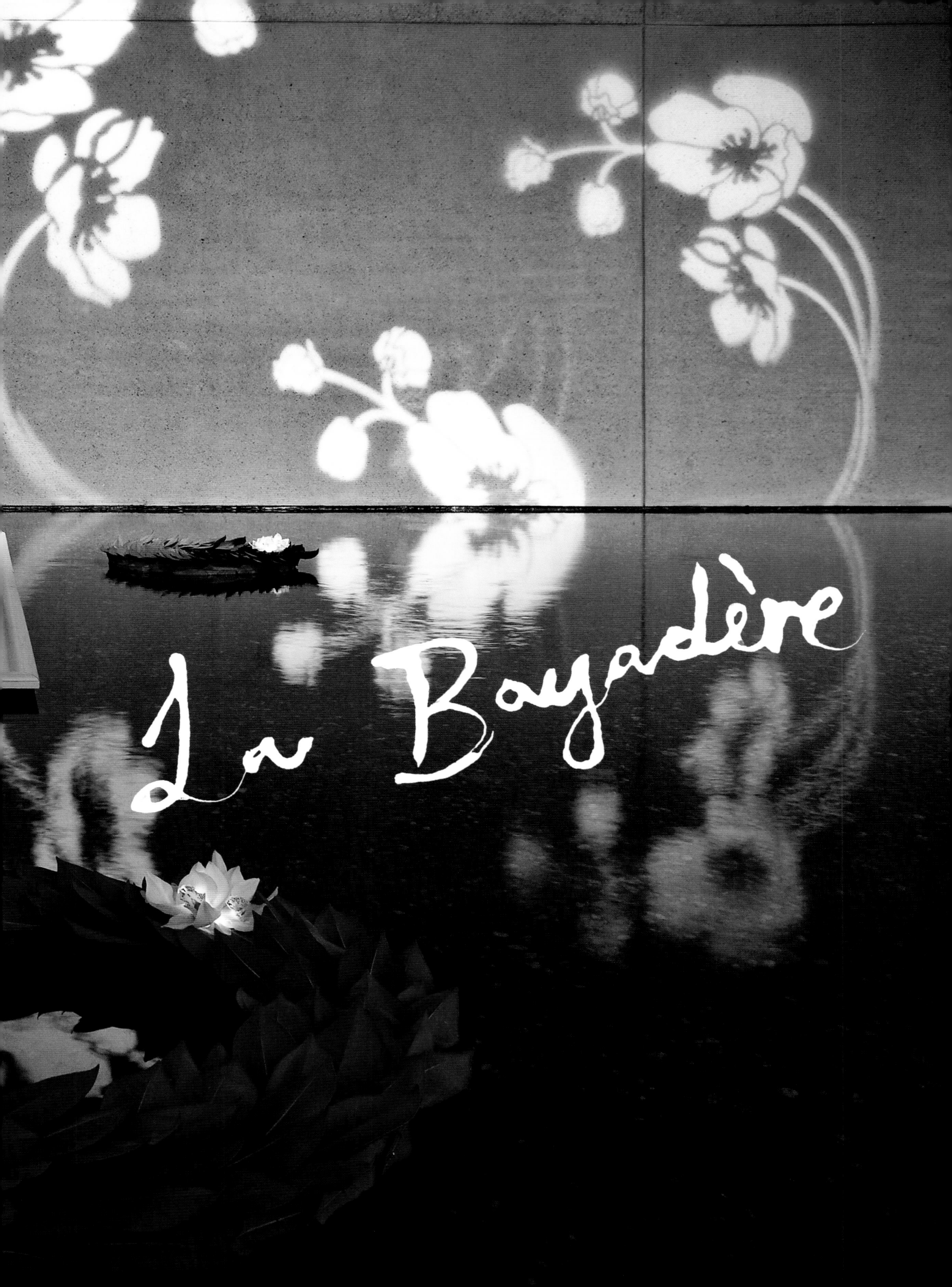
La Bayadère

Internationally renowned, the Paris Opera Ballet is the world's oldest and most influential ballet company and, for many balletomanes, the world's finest. With a permanent home in the glorious Palais Garnier, this incomparable ensemble can trace its history back to 1661, when Louis XIV founded the Académie Royale de Danse. It has nurtured many legendary dancers – including Sylvie Guillem – and influential artistic directors. Rudolf Nureyev staged superb versions of the great Russian classics for this extraordinary ensemble. This is the company's first-ever visit to Brisbane, where they will perform Marius Petipa's spectacular *La Bayadère*.

The dancers of the Paris Opera Ballet have a poise and elegance that is uniquely French, and a startling versatility that enables them to perform, with equal ease and impact, traditional nineteenth-century ballets such as *Swan Lake*, *Giselle* and *Sleeping Beauty* and challenging new works by contemporary choreographers such as Pina Bausch and Wayne McGregor. Astonishingly beautiful to watch, and with formidable technique, they have seduced audiences across the globe.

We have created floral decorations for both their recent Australian tours. For this visit, a post-performance dinner on opening night for 250 guests is being held at the new Queensland Art Gallery complex, a majestic modern sandstone building on the Brisbane River, complete with a reflection pool inside the gallery.

We create twenty-five table centrepieces in white perspex bonbon vases with ligularia, pink-edged 'Weber's Parrot' tulips and anemones the colour of Perrier-Jouët champagne, as well as ornamental fig.

We create floating garlands to place in the reflection pool. The bases are made from polystyrene wrapped in wreath wrap, which are then covered with magnolia leaves and white cymbidium orchids in clusters. We secure them with pins we've made. We have to wade into the water in gumboots to attach the garlands, weighed down by stones to keep them in place so they don't drift to the edges of the reflection pool.

They perform several pieces including Ravel's *Bolero* for the diners. And what an honour to be inspired by seeing *La Bayadère* as a conclusion to this event.

Enchanted Garden Party

During November we prepare for an event on a scale we rarely experience. It is to be a celebration; an 'evening under the stars' in a marquee in a glamorous harbourside garden. Working closely with an events management team, our job is to create feature floral decorations that will be so eye-catching and have such a strong presence that the structure of the marquee will recede from view.

We are so energised when we discuss different ideas for this job – it's a dream come true to be given such a floral adventure. After much discussion we decide to create purpose-built metal frames laden with flowers that will be suspended from the ceiling of the marquee. They will be free-floating and hang from the marquee truss on cable wire. We appreciate the faith the client has in us when we propose the idea, supported by the roughest of mock-ups, which we have put together in a matter of minutes on a market morning. They catch the vision immediately and like our 'go-forward' approach.

We need to work closely with the marquee riggers and have many meetings to determine the suspended height and sightlines. Our aim is to create a continuous arbour that seems to grow from the ground, up the marquee walls and along the roof. The construction of these floral sculptures take many extra hands, ladders and trucks. It takes three days just to bring everything in, from sandbags to large pots, buckets and boxes of flowers.

Because the event takes place in one of Sydney's hottest months, we need to consider the effect of the heat on our flowers. We choose sweet william flowers for their good texture and ability to withstand the heat, and add hydrangea and peonies at the very last minute. We cable-tie bunches of this combination onto the structures to give an abundant look.

At the entrance to the venue there is a gigantic circular table in front of a striking, coral-toned painting. As soon as I see this it is clear we have to use copious amounts of 'Coral Charm' peonies in this position. Fortunately, we have the use of an extraordinary range of vases from the client's home for our abundance of peonies. We choose deep maroon-chocolatey brown vases as well as some in pink, which complement the blooms. As we complete the arrangement, with that magnificent painting – our 'muse' – looking on, we realise that this is a moment that will never be repeated.

Felicity, our peony grower, has always loved gardening, but as an army wife she was always moving and was never able to establish a garden. She always vowed that when she retired, she would grow flowers, and her commercial peony business in Tasmania has developed from there.

Felicity is wonderfully organised and a true perfectionist, making her a dream to work with - she says this comes from both her training as a nurse, and her life as a service wife 'moving household, children, dog, cats, parrots and tropical fish from North Queensland to Hobart via Sydney, Canberra and Melbourne with side trips to Singapore. This hones organisational skills that bring about sharp disciplinary results if you fail - cooked goldfish in the back of the car!'

Peonies

Peonies have been cultivated in cold regions all over the world for both their medicinal properties and ornamental beauty. They tend to grow on open hillsides and mountains from China to the Pyrenees. In Chinese culture the peony is known as the 'King of Flowers' and the 'Flower of Riches and Honour', and symbolises beauty, love and affection.

ARCHITECTURAL
MAGNOLIA

Oh, valiant and untamed were we,
When we planted the white magnolia tree!
And the white magnolia grew and grew,
Holding our love within its core,
And every year it bloomed anew,
And we were twenty-one no more.

Helen Deutsch, 'The White Magnolia Tree'

At the late July wedding of two architects, an intimate service and lunch for thirty guests is being held. I have meetings and discussions with the clients before we create a mock-up of the event in their home. This involves taking raw materials to place in situ, suggesting flowers, vases, candles and containers, and moving things around to see how they look. We often do this for events when an unusual or more complex look is required – it's reassuring for the client to visualise exactly what they are going to receive, and for us to be safe in the knowledge that we are providing exactly what they wish, tweaking and altering until we achieve the desired effect.

We are all very inspired by a winter flowering cream magnolia, a beautiful single bloom on a leafless branch. Our other favourite is the port wine magnolia, making the basic colour scheme burgundy and cream, with hints of greens, nudes and 'Crème de Menthe' roses, using the very best of what is in season.

After agreeing on placements, I start looking for growers; one agrees that I can be there whilst he selects and handpicks the tall magnolia branches from his best trees, then collect them in the van. We'll need many branches of considerable height as the house has high ceilings.

In the entrance area, four alcoves are filled with burgundy magnolia in very tall tapered floor vases, put in place on the Thursday prior to the wedding so they open up perfectly on the day. The bridal flowers are placed in tissue-lined boxes on the suede ottoman, and a basket containing rose petals is hand-stitched with the same fabric as the bride's dress.

For the bridal table and the bouquet I use 'Queen of the Night' tulips, antique roses, kale, daphne, calla lilies, hellebores, violet leaves, anemones, ajuga leaves, artichokes, unripe green loquats and port wine magnolias.

A variety of containers are used, including tapered vases, goldfish bowls and crystal vases, as well as a few special pieces of the bride's silverware with a Perrier-Jouët theme. These are all placed on a linen runner, along with embroidered napkins from Paris and handwritten place cards. The arrangements are compact, full and structured; there are two lunch tables and, in a smaller room, a table for the children and their friends.

The mantelpiece has an arrangement of 'Crème de Menthe' roses in vases, together with antique roses. The bride's dressing-room is decorated with roses and magnolias in a glass vase, all white and elegant to go with the bridal gown.

We cut pieces of architectural tracing paper into neat squares, sticking the seam with tape. The guests are given the cones, which we fill with rose petals, to scatter at the conclusion of the wedding vows. Downstairs and outside we flutter plenty of rose petals along the stairs, their colour chosen to match the coffee-coloured bridesmaids' dresses. A large, eclectic arrangement is placed on the signing table outdoors.

Our magnolia grower Lawrence invited me to
accompany him as he hand-selected and picked
branches from his very best trees. We've
been working together ever since I started
Grandiflora. It was a big treat to visit
the property and see the magnolias growing.
We always learn a lot from our growers and
vice versa.

Lawrence and his
sister Anna grew into
their family business
— initially based on
roses, carnations and
dahlias — and started
growing magnolias, which
were quite unusual then.
He says flowers are in
their blood — a lifelong
passion.

Magnolias

A winter flowering cream magnolia.

Dreamy Barossa

Lord, make me an instrument of your peace.
Where there is hatred, let me sow love.
Where there is injury, pardon.
Where there is discord, unity.
Where there is doubt, faith.
Where there is error, truth.
Where there is despair, hope.
Where there is sadness, joy.
Where there is darkness, light.

O Divine Master, grant that I may not so much seek
to be consoled as to console
to be understood as to understand
to be loved as to love.

For

It is in giving that we receive.
It is in pardoning that we are pardoned.
It is in dying that we are born to eternal life.

The prayer of St Francis of Assissi

Approaching the Adelaide Hills I am full of both excitement and trepidation. This is a wedding for a very dear friend of mine, taking place in a brand-new venue built by the Beer family in the Barossa Valley for special events. This is the first time it will be used and I am to be both florist and guest – quite an honour. There are many willing helpers for this wedding.

The very large, sun-filled hall is wonderfully light. The last time I had seen the venue, two months prior to the wedding, it was merely a skeleton. Now I have to do some thinking on the spot.

The key words that the couple gave me were that the flowers should be 'harmonious' and 'dreamy'. The ceremony is to take place outside by the dam, complete with old wooden jetty and yabbies. The wedding party and celebrant will stand at the water's edge on a raised set of palette crates covered in hessian.

We need to make garlands of white carnations to toss over a limb of the blue gum beside which the ceremony will take place, so the night before the wedding we hold a working bee in Maggie Beer's piano room. With plenty of champagne in crystal flutes to aid our threading skills we place carnations on lengths of fishing line, knotting them so they don't all slip to one end. Delight! Music and friends and good old-fashioned fun.

We incorporate hardy and readily available flowers and foliage for this event. Local orange and pink flowering gum is cut and used in the table vases – very striking and distinct, especially at night under low light. It reminds me of little patches of fireworks.

The water of the dam, flowing from a natural spring, also reflects the soft green of the many willow and olive trees that surround it, all set against a typically blue Australian summer sky.

Maggie's olive trees, surrounding the dam, are available for us to cut from. Many of the trees are gnarled with ancient trunks. I send my companion, Gary, and his friend to cut selected branches that we will use for the table decoration. They meet with a good many red-bellied black snakes, out for a slither.

The branches we need have to be long and shapely. We use two branches in each vase for balance, and they are placed every metre along the 12-metre table. This is to make use of and provide some focus in the very large space between the tabletop and the ceiling. We remove most of the leaves from the lower part of each branch so they will not obstruct and inhibit guests talking. As a guest I find the olive branches to be fabulously overwhelming – it is rather like sitting *in* an olive grove.

We need flowers between the olive branches on the table to give colour and beauty, and it has been organised for us to use many-coloured garden roses from the local Lindeman Estate. Free to clipper what we need on the morning of the event – luxury! A florist's dream.

The central floral theme the bride has requested for the bridal party is peonies, particularly for her bouquet. They are very dark, a crimson red, tightly closed, and totally spectacular as they open, complementing her Michelle Jank dress. The bouquet lasts an astonishing ten days after the wedding.

For the flower girl, Laura, the bride's niece, mini-roses are wired into a loose circlet, multi-layered and very thick with petite flowers for her to wear on her head. As Maggie has a very fine voice, she and her choir lead us in many favourite songs.

At the very last minute we make a rose petal path for the bride to follow into the ceremonial area. A breeze comes up as I scatter the petals – they begin to flutter and spiral around playfully. I had intended a path for her to walk on, but the petals disagree, and, with the help of the breeze, they have fun turning into a gentle, unorganised snow cloud. This is what the bride remembers best of her arrival.

Fecund.
Canoe

The team at Coco Republic are indulging a group of their select clients for the launch of the inaugural Chef's Table range with an exclusive dinner and fine champagne and wines from Moet & Chandon. *Belle* magazine's interior design editor and stylist collaborate with Coco Republic and Grandiflora to transform the Coco Republic showroom in Sydney's Alexandria into a glamorous and decadent setting for a dinner party. The mood is 'luxe safari' and the colour theme is multiple green hues against hessian and silver.

Their quirky idea is to use a wooden canoe from the showroom as the major prop for our sculptural and floral installation. Suspended dramatically above the dining table, this will be the central focus of the event. Into the canoe we hoist a trailerful of green bracken fern, enormous tropical leaves and green cymbidium orchids, trailing amaranthus, sixty pots of maidenhair fern, medusa leaves, cascading cedar berry, swirling napenthe trails, and clouds of green and blue hydrangeas.

Working out quantities for very large installations is one of the first priorities in a job like this, as so much importance rests on it – from the availability of the materials and the cost to the client to the look of the arrangement. Measurements need to be taken of the vessel, and the choice, amount and scale of the material is all considered to give the greatest impact.

We need to do a lot of styling, using selected props. Most of the guests are interior designers and decorators and we imagine they will be very visual people, observing all the small details. The dining table needs to be understated. We use rare 'Green Trick' carnations, placed directly on to the table to echo moss mounds, velvet leaves and other very rare leaf specimens and white phalaenopsis orchids set amongst sculptural silver candlesticks and smoked glass tea-light candle holders, both complete with beeswax candles. Individual succulents, which need a lot of cleaning beforehand, sit on miniature tropical leaves for each guest's place setting, eventually to be taken home and – we hope – planted as a memento of the evening. This is a wonderful way of adding generosity, interest and elegance to the table, whilst not disturbing the central floral decoration.

After an event using such large quantities, the client will quite often keep the flowers afterwards or we donate them to hospitals, nursing homes or schools.

Casino Royale

We are invited to be involved in one of Australia's premier awards nights, the Logies. Our client has a very clear vision and directive, requiring us to source vast quantities of flowers in particular shades from Melbourne growners. The tulips exceed our wildest expectations, more than appropriate for the grand ballroom of the Crown Casino. For this project we are surprised to be working in the foyer with Annie Lennox rehearsing nearby! The casino is a real labyrinth and we need a lot of trolleys to move the flowers close to our work area. A full security check is necessary; we are given reflective jackets to wear and an official ID, but everyone is very friendly and extremely helpful.

We gain inspiration for this event from a painting in the casino's collection: overlaying dark lines suggesting an angular figure on a delicate gradation of soft grey background colour, using much delicate pink. We use masses of pink flowers, predominantly lisianthus and tulips, in bunches. They speak for themselves without the need for complicated arranging. Huge individual rose heads go in mini goldfish bowls, while vanda orchid stems are placed in specimen vases for height. They are very photogenic and will work well on TV, as they add dimension to the table. A lot of pink filtered lighting is used to create a soft, relaxed atmosphere.

Because of the size of this event we need to order the raw materials well in advance to be sure enough 'Rosalie' tulips have been grown, and order the cut flowers at least three weeks ahead. Shopping at the Melbourne market is a very different experience to the crazy, rushed atmosphere of the Sydney market, as the general public are not allowed in to shop during trade shopping time. Their chrysanthemum disbuds are the best in Australia – this is a technique where growers discard most of the buds while they grow, leaving one special bloom at the top that receives all the nutrition and eventually becomes enormous and very impressive. I can never pass a grower and not buy them.

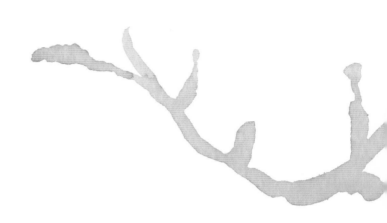

THE
GOLDEN BIRD

Il mattino ha l'oro in bocca.
(The morning has gold in its mouth.)
Italian proverb

Designers are among our most regular clients, and they are often very inspired by flowers. A prominent French clothing label invite us to turn a private viewing of their new collection into something extraordinary.

Invitations are sent out to fashion buyers for a special dinner at an elegant 1920s Potts Point terrace house. In days gone by, this building housed a chic French restaurant. Now it is a photographic studio and an ideal event location, with its ornate high ceilings, white walls and polished floorboards. We place bentwood bistro chairs, a long table and wonderful French antiques from Sydney-based interiors store The Country Trader around the room.

At the first concept meeting with the client we are shown the invitation for the event, which features an image of a large yellow flower, and decide to use this as our inspiration. The client has also decided they want live canaries in the main room, so yellow is the theme of the day. Vibrant and evocative, yellow has an imposing presence, like the intense summer sun. I'm reminded of my great-aunt Elsa saying 'Look to the sun and laugh, for the strength of the morning is yours.' With the colour theme decided, we know that poppies are a must, as they come in an enormous variety of yellows, from pale to brilliant.

Instead of bringing finished arrangements to the venue, we prepare it all in situ, adding and removing as we go along. This way we are able to respond to the venue's interiors and create a relaxed look without it feeling 'over-arranged'.

The main display sits in a magnificent ceramic urn on a grand sideboard. It stands before a very large mirror, which gives it even more gravitas. This large arrangement starts with a base of silver suede leaf, then, one by one, we place different flowers in random positions against the foliage, being careful to balance the colour.

When I arrange like this, I feel like an artist layering colour on a canvas, building up the final image.

Kaleidoscope
Clutch

A friend and client, accessories designer Rachael Ruddick, suggests we collaborate on a collection and I leap at the idea: very colourful, elegant small clutch purses. It becomes a botanical collection of clutch bags, in fabric designed for three colourways: yellow/orange, blue/purple and silvery grey.

To create the designs, we place flowers on a very long oasis sheet on the floor, in the selected colours, flowerheads only, tightly packed, dense and half-open, picked for the colour with fleshy petals for strength. These are photographed from above at quite a height. Rachael takes over from here with the design and making of the bags. The photographs are then made into photo stencils for silk screens, and printed on to silk fabric.

We have a launch at Grandiflora. Clients are surprised and delighted at the sight of a bag launch in amongst so many flowers complete with waiters and guests sipping drinks and eating. We decorate the studio with a lot of vibrant colour at the front – peonies, tulips, lilies, spring blossom and miltonia orchids – changing colour towards the back of the shop to green, silver and grey, more foliage and leaves. We line one whole wall with very tall macrocarpa branches and huge green leaves. There are also small groups of multicoloured, handcrafted silk beetles alighting on leaves, flowers and bags.

The guests are served rose-petal tea and violet soda, profiteroles with mini roses on top and lavender meringues. What a beautiful floral affair. The studio feels so crisp, green and clean – the display on our central workbench is quite scientific-looking, with vases turned upside down, bag specimens encased inside them, one stacked on top of another. The clutch purses have since become collectors' items.

A Rabble of Butterflies

A St Mary's Cathedral wedding followed by a lunch reception at the Museum of Contemporary Art (MCA), on the harbour, facing the Sydney Opera House – an unsurpassable setting for a magic winter wedding. Sydney is treating our clients to one of its most perfect days: a crisp, sunny July Saturday.

We have worked very closely with an events co-ordinator to prepare for this wedding, her inspiration coming from the Peranaken aesthetic, a Chinese culture that emphasises ritual and ceremony and includes lots of intricately embroidered clothing. We only meet the bride once and her directive is simply, 'I trust you to do a beautiful job!'.

We need to move quickly between the venues. To decorate the cathedral, we place four tapered 8-foot-high pots with flowering white camellia trees either side of the central aisle, containing roses together with bare magnolia branches and camellias that are decorated with many, many decorative feather butterflies and garlands.

We bend and manoeuvre the trees in the central aisle towards each other to form an arch, and add garlands of white Singapore orchids and clusters of sweet peas throughout the low branches, as well as bundles of white roses tucked down into the base of each pot. Cream cymbidium orchids are placed in the front urns to add further glamour. White butterflies hang from the huge camellia branches, creating a very pretty overhead garland, and look almost like flowers themselves.

A sole female voice begins to sing 'Ave Maria' and my eyes start to moisten. The bride and her maids each carry a hand-crafted 'hybrid' flower consisting of orchid petals. These are very labour-intensive to make.

The room at the MCA is huge, with a 7-metre-high ceiling, so we need to make it feel more intimate. We wrap the ceiling beams in cloth to minimise their presence. There will be twenty-five tables, both round and oblong, plus the bridal table.

To create each arrangement we begin with a magnolia branch, in bud, sturdy and well developed. To this we entwine, wrap and lash many flowers in garlands, adding peppercorn, white Singapore orchids, cymbidiums in sprays, lengths of crystals, ornate bird cages and silk butterflies. We need three separate rigs on motors with which to hoist each arrangement to an area midway between tabletops and ceiling.

The chair covers are white organdie with butterfly motifs and the tablecloths are pale grey with borders of silver brocade. The table settings include delicate Chinese crockery, teapots, oriental cups and saucers, and a present for everyone of a loose single cymbidium orchid bloom at each setting. The table centres are decorated with tightly bunched, short-stemmed white and pale pink roses, white roses with red outer petals, roses and sweet peas; the flowers are to be taken home by the guests following the reception.

We use lighting to create the impression of going from daylight into night-time ambience, hoping light will bounce off everything in a gentle ricochet around the room. Ceiling spot lights complement beeswax candles flickering through suspended strands of multi-faceted crystals.

The first impression on entering the area is acres and acres of flowers and beauty.

Close to the entrance is a Peranakan 'message tree'. It suggests that guests take a butterfly card and envelope from the tree, write a message of goodwill for the bridal couple and re-hang it; also on the tree are hanging glass bowls with single rose or camellia heads inside.

a Rondo of Roses

Men do a lot of flower shopping on Valentine's Day and each year there are some very grand, over-the-top expressions of love made for someone important in the life of the giver.

One such expression will always stay in my mind. A gentleman called from London; he was wooing a woman he had met in Sydney and was trying to persuade her to meet him in London.

Willing to pay all expenses, he wanted to fill her office with pink roses before she arrived at work. We secretly contacted her assistant to open the office early, enabling us to install the copious stems. We used glass vases en masse. The recipient rang as soon as she arrived as she was so overwhelmed. And all her friends were very jealous!

Another memorable Valentine sent a bunch of roses on the hour, every hour, all day. We had to be very clever with our deliveries to make sure we were prompt – I think the recipient was quite exhilarated by the last delivery!

And my very favourite Valentine's message that I've ever attached to a bunch of blooms? 'You are the ginger in my sushi.'

Nature Reloaded

The Palm House in Sydney's Royal Botanic Gardens provides a very charming venue for many occasions and exhibitions. It is unique in Sydney because it offers a blank canvas with very few facilities – so in essence the client can make it their own.

Launching the new season's collection of jewels, we are hoping to create a sophisticated, elegant ambience with a touch of the exotic. Guests include buyers from the fashion industry. Featuring are three gorgeous, full-size stuffed peacocks, and five glass bell jars with large butterflies inside, providing very strong flashes of turquoise, brilliant blue and gold, complementing the peacocks' colour and the sparkle of crystals.

We place large mirrored pedestals along the centre of the hall, together with lower mirrored cubes to give tiered height. On these stands we place glass specimen vases and flutes. Between the vases, covetable rings, bracelets, necklaces, clutch bags and watches, meticulously manoeuvred

into our installation, are threaded. We take our inspiration for the colours from the jewels. In these we place cattleya and vanda orchids, napenthe trails, saracenias, special tropical leaves, venus flytraps, callicarpa and a beaded branch of pink berries. The mirrored plinths reflect it all and create a multi-faceted illusion.

To make the space feel more intimate and create atmosphere, we fill the ceiling area by strapping huge quantities of tall, leafless magnolia branches to the rafters, interspersed with bunches of open tulips in strong colours, petals flipped back to give them a more open appearance.

We suspend crystal strands from the branches to look like a waterfall, with trailing small-leaved greenery and bracken fern. To complete the show, the back wall of the hall displays a large digital floral image, clusters of tulips along the ceiling rafters echoing its colour. This is nature enhanced, gilded – and reloaded.

'Nature reloaded' – an explosion of colour and glittering light, with flowers, mirrors, crystals, birds and butterflies all enhancing each other's beauty.

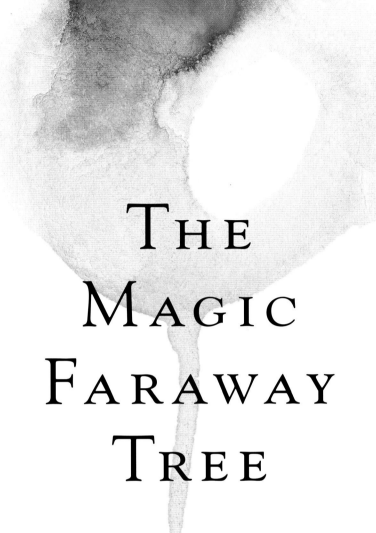

THE MAGIC FARAWAY TREE

Fairfax and Roberts is Australia's oldest bespoke jeweller, established in 1858 and still at the forefront of jewellery design, with signature ranges developed by celebrated designer Michelle Jank, and more to come under the wing of new creative director Thierry Martin.

To launch their new collection, with only three days' notice we decide to recreate a huge romantic cherry blossom tree in the centre of their showroom. This will provide the setting for the launch breakfast. The beautiful, elegant space with its extremely high ceiling provides a magnificent backdrop for our tree.

We start with a 6-metre-high pole to which we strap hessian, green moss, tarpa cloth, palm husks and grey lichen in differing thicknesses to create a trunk. This trunk proves to be highly challenging, with our producer getting nervous. There is much wrapping and forming and, when it's finished, it looks not unlike a Moreton Bay fig.

After many trips up and down the scaffold, the trunk soon evolves into a flowering cherry tree. We use bundles of magnolia and jacaranda branches, which are delivered straight from the grower to the venue. We're so lucky to have such good service at such late notice! To the branches we cable-tie long stems of sweet peas, and irregular bunches of peach and cherry blossom, all in varying shades of pink. These branches and flowers all cascade, trail and flow from the ceiling towards the ground. It is light, open and magic.

Everlasting
Australiana

This is to be a seated dinner for approximately one hundred people at Government House in Sydney. Its striking sandstone walls, its deep sense of history and its setting in beautiful Bennelong Point, in the middle of Sydney's Royal Botanic Gardens, make it a dream venue. The director has asked us to work with the concept of 'Australiana'.

We use colourful natives for the table centrepiece which are in fact two very long (20-metre) garlands consisting of large-petal flannel flowers in clusters – bunching them gives form to this soft, often delicate, ancient flower – as well as pinwheels and gum blossom with large decorative gumnuts. These garlands are made onsite on a base of hessian gardening tape; working on the spot gives a fresher, more harmonious look. At each place setting we lay a small bouquet of native orange daisies. We also fill two large containers on the stage with natives featuring large leaves and pink gum blossom together with their seed pods.

The spirit of Bennelong watches over us, recalling our shared history with the Aboriginal people. This area has been home to the Cadigal people for many thousands of years and remains a site of spiritual significance today.

These dinners facilitate contact with benefactors, without whom many historic houses, with their excellent guardianship of Sydney's past, would have difficulty surviving.

For this all-white fashion shoot, we create floral adornments on the spot, working quickly to combat the heat. Babies' breath, daisies and roses complement the tutus, feathered headdress, beekeepers' outfit and even a white horse.

Fantasia

Driving through Centennial Park on this beautiful Sunday morning, you might think you had stumbled upon a Fellini film set. This is an epic photoshoot inspired by the Disney movie *Fantasia* and interpreted by the designer Michelle Jank, and the guests/ extras have been given one directive: dress in white only, anything white – even bring a white pet if you have one.

The effect is theatrical in the extreme: long trailing, floating dresses; lace; velvet cloaks; shorter than short mini everything; tulle and ballet-like creations; gleaming white patent leather stilt shoes; leather skirts, shorts and shoes; white dogs, kittens and a horse; satin; organza; top hats; a full-length white feather Indian headdress; bonnets and a hat with a cockade. Someone wears a white rabbit suit, although it is a very hot day – the mermaid looks much cooler. There's plenty of exotic make-up and decorative parasols – even a bee-keeper and an astronaut. An all-white fantasy gathering with a space-age model dressed by Michelle, epitomising the future of fashion.

We are decorating people's outfits with white flowers, using our van as an air-conditioned, portable flower studio. Step right up and let our team create something to adorn your outfit on the spot! Pins and ribbons fly in every direction; we have a line of fashionistas queuing for flowers.

We come up with plenty of fanciful creations, notably a very large headpiece made from white hydrangeas. White babies' breath cascades over Jenny Kee's and Linda Jackson's organdie lace gowns; we make necklaces like ruffles from roses and lisianthus all in white, and wristlets from phalaenopsis orchids. Making the feature neck arrangement for Michelle is our most essential concern; we thread flowers into garlands, and wind the long strands around and around her neck to create a breastplate of undulating blooms. A lot of water and constant spraying is needed in the open heat. This is a full-scale production – a real happening.

Violetta Valediction

A few years ago I drove past a very dramatic cemetery on a headland overlooking the ocean. 'That's just the spot for me,' I thought. So I wrote to the local council to ask how to reserve a plot. They wrote back saying 'Contact us closer to the time.' Lately I have been thinking about my own funeral, as have other friends. It's quite common to have it on your mind, I expect, if you are a florist, as we deal with this part of life often in our work.

Funerals vary enormously; they are very personal and reflect the deceased. Unusual items are often included due to their significance in the life of the person. Pure white single roses are often used for very young people. At a prominent Australian artist's funeral there was a hand-painted casket, decorated by his family using native bush flowers, birds and plants, relating to the environment that he lived in. A glorious visual feast.

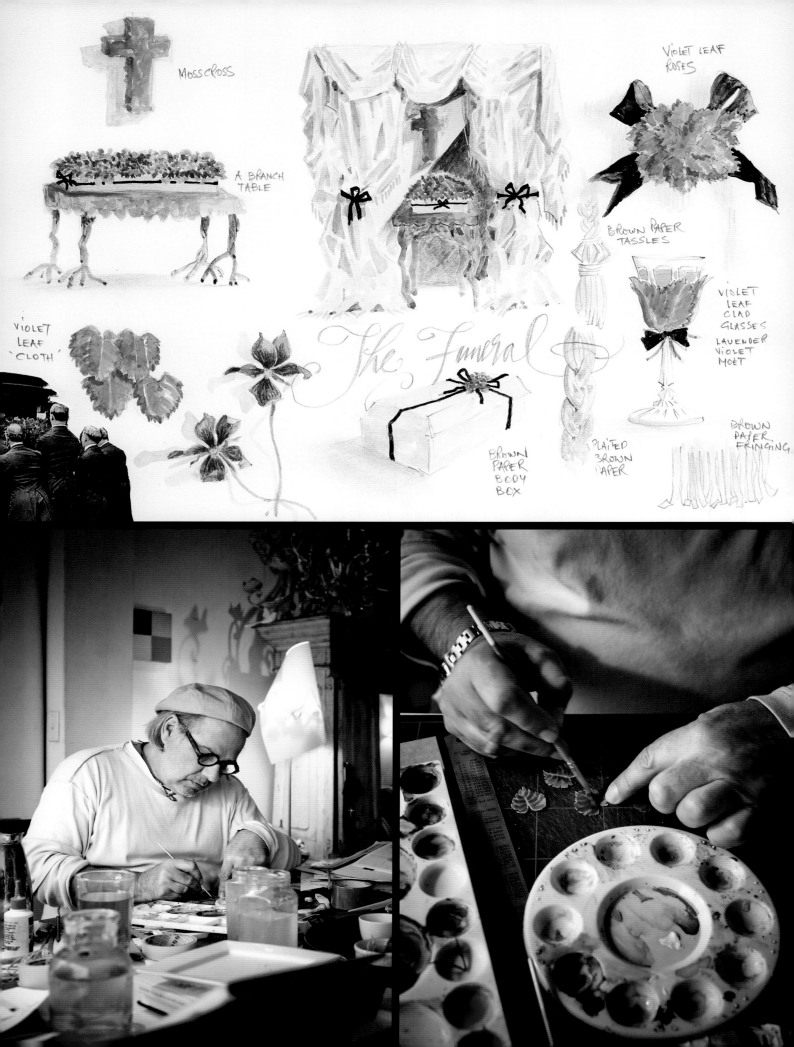

MOSS CROSS

A BRANCH TABLE

VIOLET LEAF ROSES

BROWN PAPER TASSLES

VIOLET LEAF 'CLOTH'

VIOLET LEAF CLAD GLASSES

LAVENDER VIOLET MOËT

The Funeral

BROWN PAPER BODY BOX

PLAITED BROWN PAPER

BROWN PAPER FRINGING

Recently at a funeral at St Mary's Cathedral in Sydney, those attending were asked to carry a branch of jacaranda. Every November when the jacarandas bloom, they now evoke a personal memory for those who attended. On occasion funerals are as highly orchestrated as weddings.

James Gordon, renowned events stylist, watercolourist and designer has completely designed his own funeral, creating a diorama of a beautiful chapel, and setting down all his ideas as detailed illustrations on paper.

Violets are his great love and he hopes for them to be in a soft hedge formation on the casket top, thickly bunched and set in a bed of moss. Delicate, perfumed and reminiscent of past times.

James says: 'Somewhere in Italy and some time ago, I came across a simple stone chapel on a lonely road. The interior was stark in its beauty. Windows of clear glass, no pews; a beaten-up old oak table was the pulpit. Rush-seated oak chairs were stacked in rough rows and the sun beamed in, in beautiful shafts.

'In the shadows, and in a gap in the wall where a stone was missing, I saw a plain cross made of twigs above an old anchovy jar filled with deepest purple violets. It was the loveliest of images and will never leave me.

'I've loved violets since I watched my dear old Aunt Mary embroider them on to pillowcases; I was probably five. Aunt Mary grew violets in her tiny garden at Marrickville and we both waited each year until they peeped open.

'I paint violets; I collect any fragrance, oil or candle that has a violet note. My very favourite Dyptique perfume, "Violetta", has sadly been discontinued, but I still have a few drops left for special occasions.

'I've always liked brown paper. The colour, the simplicity and the many uses it has; with the purple of violets it is, for me, near perfection.

'My diorama is based on all the above. The floor and walls are made from paper, as is the coffin; the legs of the funeral table are chicken bones, the violets are cut from paper and detailed in gouache.

'As violets only bloom in winter, clearly I need to drop down dead in August if I really want this funeral look; although more important to me is my wake that I plan to have before I go and this shall occur in an August of my choice.'

A Head Full of Colour

'Come to the edge!'
'We can't, we're afraid!'
'Come to the edge.'
'We can't, we will fall!'
'Come to the edge,' and they came
and he pushed them
and they flew.

Christopher Logue, 'Come to the edge'

Montalbetti and Campbell are a photographic duo originating from Canada who work within the fashion world but branch out into exceptional, creative large-format colour exhibition photographs, featuring obvious references to old masterpieces and fashion from many eras. Their work is sensual, 'drunk on beauty', and uses flowers and floral decoration to astonishing effect.

For their exhibition opening at the Australian Centre for Photography, a dinner and fashion show are held. It features two models, creating a very potent performance. Styled by Kelvin Harries, they saunter through the dining crowd in beautifully chosen jackets, puffed skirts and intricate blouses with elaborate ruffles and buttons, very high shoes and powerful make-up.

We create floral headpieces with neck and wrist decorations to match; colour is to feature largely, as well as form. We've determined we won't make these flowers too pretty, but more directional and blocked, with strength in numbers of blooms, plus serious colour. The headpieces are lashed on with skewers, leaving the netting they're attached to exposed. The models bravely endure the weaving, skewering and wiring until they look beyond spectacular. Lisianthus and carnations provide strong exotic purple, while intense red is created by roses and peonies, with yellow touches provided by more peonies and freesias. As we leave we spot the poem by Christopher Logue, and feel completely inspired to spread our wings.

A Gingerbread House in the Woods

The Waring family's Christmas tree-growing business is based in what looks like the original 'gingerbread house in the woods', although being Australian, of course it's really a log cabin in the bush. Originally from Canberra, the family moved to Robertson in the southern highlands of New South Wales as they felt drawn to the land and this property in particular.

Ten years after first being invited, I finally make it there for morning tea, and what a tea it is – handmade scones, knitted tea cosies, many photos to look at and numerous family stories. I find myself wishing I had more time! I have to leave partway through to watch my daughter Ginger do her end-of-year dressage test, but on my return I am taken on a full-scale tour of the property. It's all in the cause of securing the perfect Christmas trees to be decorated by Grandiflora.

The Warings started their business when they found that the Australian German community, including the Lutheran church, preferred real fir Christmas trees with perfect 360-degree symmetry – scarce in Australia in those days. Their passion has been passed down to the next generation. Their trees are a very even shape with a symmetrical branch pattern – the quintessential Grimm Brothers' fairytale Christmas trees. The Warings planted a forest – it is now an intense sea of green fir! Clients come to look and select the tree of their choice.

To create a formal traditional Christmas tree I use green pine cones, tea light candles in suspended glass bowls, fairy lights threaded through the branches and small bundles of gardenia and magnolia blooms woven through the decorations. We also make Christmas wreaths with fir and succulents from a base of rainforest vines. We make them to order according to the client's wishes – sometimes, the previous year's wreaths are returned and we strip them back to their original base and start from scratch, with groupings of elements wired or cable-tied on to the base.

Our Christmas tree growers, the Warings, are based on a beautiful
12-hectare property, situated next to a picturesque cemetery.
Their trees are visible in the background in some scenes of
the movie 'Babe', which was shot on the property next door.
The rich red basalt soil and high rainfall in the area make
ideal growing conditions.

The family has been in the business since 1964. I met them after
I'd been phoning around for two days solid, looking for a tree
for one of our VIP clients.

They originally started growing
the trees for timber, but noticed
that the young ones made attractive
Christmas trees. They grow both
blue spruce and Douglas fir trees,
which look very similar to the
traditional European Christmas
trees. They appealed to the many
European workers in the Wollongong
area, who wanted a reminder of
home at Christmas time.

The trees take between eight and ten years to grow to a good size for harvesting, and some of them are fifteen years old at harvest time. The firs need to be pruned to make sure they are an attractive shape, whereas the blue spruces grow naturally into a perfect Christmas-tree shape. When the Warings harvest, they try to leave some lower branches on the stump, which are then 'trained' up to become two new trees. This takes around five or six years. Some stumps have produced four or five trees and are still going.

Christmas Trees

In Appreciation

Louise Havekes Walker
Julie Gibbs
Arielle Gamble
Jocelyn Hungerford
Daniel New
Ingrid Ohlsson
Ariane Durkin
Virginia Birch
Erin Langlands
Julia Parker
Sean Cook
Johanna Detmold
May Lloyd
Grace Morley
Justine Hasselton
Lisa Cooper
Lucinda Johnson
Renee Wierzbicki
Greg Samson

CREDITS

We would like to thank the following for their generous assistance with this book.

Introduction
Ineke Souris: *Saskia and Flowers*
The Art Gallery of NSW
Louis MacNeice
Faber and Faber

Life in Abundance
Kylie Kwong
Paul Kwong
Kin Chen
Gemma Whiteman
Louise Olsen and
Stephen Ormandy

Lotuses
Steve Spartalis of Plant Space

**Doilies & Pearls,
Oysters & Shells**
Romance Was Born
Mark Vassallo
Phillip Skelton and Sam Borridge –
Hot Sets, Sun Studios

Epiphany
Andrew and Caroline Moffitt

A Tower of Teacups
Sharyn Storrier Lyneham and EDIT
Luke Storrier Lyneham

Hydrangeas
Serena Coppolino

Raise the Red Ribbon
dg3

Paradise Found
All the staff at Cocoa Island

Orchid Feast
Gowan Stewart

Orchids
Gowan Stewart .

The Blush of Youth
TP Events

Fragrant Falling
Sisley
Star PR
Art Gallery of New South Wales

Sweet Avalanche
Marie Claire
dg3

Strapping Macrocarpa
David Jones
Team Event

**By the Willow, in the Rain,
in the Evening**
Kit Podgornik
Maree Andrews

Our Lady of the Camellias
Johanna and Ged Verus

Camellias
Camellia Grove

Radiant Sister of the Day
Harper's Bazaar
Mark Vassallo
Miranda Kerr

The Scarlet Pimpernel
Black Communications
Country Trader

Foraging Tussy-Mussy
Mayfield Gardens
Erika Lynn
Mr and Mrs Fish

Dahlias
Barry Willard

Roses en Pointe
The National Gallery of Australia,
Canberra
AGB Events Pty Ltd

Wings of Poetry
Swarovski
AWPR

Trailing, Creeping, Growing
Mrs Christina Ong
Everyone at Club 21

Spice Mural
BTTB Pty Ltd

A Rose Is a Rose Is a Rose
TP Events
Megan Morton

Roses
Paula Burchell

Technicolour Dreamers
The Art Gallery of NSW
Workshop Events

Centre Stage
Sydney Theatre Company

Royal Purple
Hermès
AWPR
Guillaume at Bennelong

Blossom High
Andrew Wilson and
Alexandra Gordon
The Wharf Restaurant

La Bayadère
Paris Opera Ballet
Leo Schofield
Janet Pankoff
QPAC
Queensland Art Gallery

Enchanted Garden Party
TP Events
Tim McGuire

Peonies
Felicity Langley

Architectural Magnolia
Allan and Naomi Stevens

Magnolias
Anna Leoncino
Lawrence Leoncino

Dreamy Barossa
The Beer Family
Adelaide Flower House

Fecund Canoe
Coco Republic
Belle
Imogen Naylor
Steve Cordony

Casino Royale
dg3

The Golden Bird
The Aesthetics Group

Kaleidoscope Clutch
James Gordon
Rachael Ruddick

A Rabble of Butterflies
Verity Roberts
Beverley Gibson
Michelle Cambridge
David Berger

A Rondo of Roses
Burley Katon Halliday

Nature Reloaded
Swarovski
AWPR
Alexandra Gordon

The Magic Faraway Tree
Fairfax & Roberts
dg3

Everlasting Australiana
Historic Houses Trust
Government House

Fantasia
Harper's Bazaar
Michelle Jank
Edward Davidson

Violetta Valediction
WN Bull Funerals
James Gordon

A Head Full of Colour
Kelvin Harries
Australian Centre for Photography

**A Gingerbread House
in the Woods**
The Szangolies Family
The Waring Family

Christmas Trees
Hugh, Roger and Brett Waring

The State Theatre

PLANT LIST

Frontispiece

Amaranthus	*Amaranthus caudatus*
Caladium	*Caladium* sp.
Clethra	*Clethra arborea*
Dutchman's Pipe	*Aristolochia* sp.
Gloriosa Lily	*Gloriosa superba*
Hoya	*Hoya* sp.
Magnolia 'Little Gem'	*Magnolia grandiflora* 'Little Gem'
Paper Daisies	*Xerochrysum bracteatum*
Plumbago	*Plumbago auriculata*
Queen Anne's Lace	*Ammi majus*
Rose	*Rosa* sp.
Seaside Daisy	*Erigeron karvinskianum*
Spinifex	*Spinifex* sp.
Thunbergia	*Thunbergia* sp.

Life in Abundance pp4–9

Alocasia	*Alocasia* sp.
Cattleya Orchid	*Cattleya* sp.
Cordyline	*Cordyline* sp.
Dendrobium Orchid	*Dendrobium* sp.
Elephant's Ear	*Xanthosoma* sp.
Emerald Duke Philodendron	*Philodendron* 'Emerald Duke'
Frangipani	*Plumeria rubra*
Lotus	*Nelumbo nucifera*
Lotus 'Hindu'	*Nelumbo* 'Hindu'
Lotus 'Mrs Perry D. Slocum'	*Nelumbo* 'Mrs Perry D. Slocum'
Medusa	*Anthurium vittariifolium*
Nepenthes	*Nepenthes* sp.
Philodendron	*Philodendron* sp.
Rock Orchid	*Dendrobium* sp.
Sherry Baby Orchid	*Oncidium* 'Sherry Baby'
Slipper Orchid	*Paphiopedilum* sp.
Turtle Leaf	*Anthurium crystallinum*
Vanda Orchid	*Vanda* sp.
Water Lily	*Nymphaea* sp.

Lotuses pp10–11

Lotus	*Nelumbo nucifera*
Lotus 'Hindu'	*Nelumbo* 'Hindu'
Lotus 'Mrs Perry D. Slocum'	*Nelumbo* 'Mrs Perry D. Slocum'

Doilies & Pearls, Oysters & Shells pp12–21

Amaranthus	*Amaranthus caudatus*
Baby's Breath	*Gypsophila paniculata*
Bracken Fern	*Pteridium esculentum*
Carnation	*Dianthus barbatus* cv.
Chrysanthemum	*Chrysanthemum* sp.
Cyclamen	*Cyclamen* sp.
Delphinium	*Delphinium* sp.
Hydrangea	*Hydrangea macrophylla* cv.
Pansy	*Viola* sp.
Plumbago	*Plumbago auriculata*
Rose 'Cecile Brunner'	*Rosa* 'Cecile Brunner'
Rosehip	*Rosa* sp.
Rosemary	*Rosmarinus officinalis*

Epiphany pp22–29

Chrysanthemum	*Chrysanthemum* sp.
Cyclamen	*Cyclamen* sp.
Hydrangea	*Hydrangea*
Hydrangea	*Hydrangea macrophylla* cv.
Pansy	*Viola* sp.
Peony	*Paeonia* sp.
Rose	*Rosa David Austen* cv.
Singapore Orchid	*Dendrobium* sp.
Strawberry	*Fragaria* x *ananassa*

A Tower of Teacups pp30–37

Hydrangea	*Hydrangea macrophylla* cv.
Rose	*Rosa David Austen* cv.
Rose	*Rosa* sp.
Violet	*Viola odorata*

Hydrangeas pp38–39

Hydrangeas	*Hydrangea macrophylla* cvs.

Raise the Red Ribbon pp40–45

Hydrangea	*Hydrangea macrophylla* cv.
Passionfruit	*Passiflora edulis*
Peony	*Paeonia* sp.

Paradise Found pp46–55

Anthurium	*Anthurium* sp.
Chrysanthemum	*Chrysanthemum* sp.
Coconut Palm	*Cocos nucifera*
Magnolia	*Magnolia* sp.
Monstera	*Monstera deliciosa*
Phalaenopsis Orchid	*Phalaenopsis* sp.
Singapore Orchid	*Dendrobium* sp.

Orchid Feast pp56–59

Cattleya Orchid	*Cattleya* sp.
Dendrobium Orchid	*Dendrobium* sp.
Oncidium Orchids	*Oncidium* sp.
Phalaenopsis Orchid	*Phalaenopsis* sp.
Sherry Baby Orchid	*Oncidium* 'Sherry Baby'
Vanda Orchid	*Vanda* sp.

Orchids pp60–61

Angraecum Orchid	*Angraecum* sp.
Cattleya Orchid	*Cattleya purpurata* syn. *Laelia purpurata*
Cattleya Orchid	*Cattleya* sp.
Crucifix Orchid	*Epidendrum* sp.
New Guinea Dendrobiums	*Dendrobium* spp.
Oncidium Orchid	*Oncidium* sp.
Phalaenopsis Orchid	*Phalaenopsis pulcherrima* syn. *Doritis pulcherrima*

The Blush of Youth pp62–67

Alocasia	*Alocasia* sp.
Anthurium	*Anthurium* sp.
Emerald Duke Philodendron	*Philodendron* 'Emerald Duke'
Lime	*Citrus aurantiifolia*
Peony	*Paeonia* sp.
Pilea	*Pilea* sp.
Rose	*Rosa* sp.

Peony Paeonia sp.
Phalaenopsis Orchid Phalaenopsis sp.
Ranunculus Ranunculus asiaticus cv.
Rice Flower Ozothamnus diosmifolius
Rose Rosa sp.
Statice Limonium sp.
Tuberose Polianthes tuberosa
Tulip Tulipa sp.

Spice Mural pp134–139

Bixa	*Bixa orellana*
Broom	*Cytisus scoparius*
Celosia	*Celosia* sp.
Cordyline	*Cordyline* sp.
Croton	*Croton* sp.
Crucifix Orchid	*Epidendrum* sp.
Cymbidium Orchid	*Cymbidium* sp.
Elephant's Ear	*Xanthosoma* sp.
Lotus	*Nelumbo nucifera*
Orange	*Citrus sinensis*
Paprika	*Capsicum annuum* cv.
Rose	*Rosa* sp.
Saffron Crocus	*Crocus sativus*
Spider Orchid	*Dendrobium* sp.
Sweet William	*Dianthus barbatus* cv.
Tortured Willow/Twisted Willow	*Salix babylonica* var.
pekinensis	'Tortuosa'
Vanda Orchid	*Vanda* sp.

A Rose Is a Rose Is a Rose pp140–147

Peppercorn Tree	*Schinus molle*
Pomegranate	*Punica granatum*
Rose	*Rosa* sp.
Tulip	*Tulipa* sp.

Roses pp148–149

Rose 'Birmingham Post	*Rosa* 'Birmingham Post
Rose 'Charles de Gaulle'	*Rosa* 'Charles de Gaulle'
Rose 'Chartreuse de Parme'	*Rosa* 'Chartreuse de Parme'
Rose 'Evelyn'	*Rosa* 'Evelyn'
Rose 'Grand Siecle'	*Rosa* 'Grand Siecle'
Rose 'Poetry'	*Rosa* 'Poetry'
Rose 'Spirit of Peace'	*Rosa* 'Spirit of Peace'
Rose 'The Children's Rose'	*Rosa* 'The Children's Rose'
Rose 'Valencia'	*Rosa* 'Valencia'
Rose	*Rosa* sp.

Technicolour Dreamers pp150–153

Carnation	*Dianthus barbatus* cv.
Chrysanthemum	*Chrysanthemum* sp.
Gerbera	*Gerbera* sp.
Hops	*Humulus lupulus*
Maiden Hair Fern	*Adiantum* sp.
Ranunculus	*Ranunculus asiaticus* cv.
Rose	*Rosa* sp.

Centre Stage pp154–159

Phalaenopsis Orchid	*Phalaenopsis* sp.
Pilea	*Pilea* sp.
Rose	*Rosa* sp.

Royal Purple pp160–163

Amaranthus	*Amaranthus caudatus*
Asparagus Fern	*Asparagus* sp.
Calla Lily	*Zantedeschia aethiopica*
Celosia	*Celosia* sp.
Fig	*Ficus carica*
Hydrangea	*Hydrangea macrophylla* cv.
Lily	*Lilium* sp.
Peony	*Paeonia* sp.
Phalaenopsis Orchid	*Phalaenopsis* sp.
Rose	*Rosa* sp.
Tulip 'Queen of the Night'	*Tulipa* 'Queen of the Night'
Vanda Orchid	*Vanda* sp.

Blossom High pp164–171

Anemone	*Anemone coronaria* cv.
Blossom	*Prunus* sp.
Camellia	*Camellia* sp.
Freesia	*Freesia* sp.
Hellebore Rose	*Helleborus* sp.
Jasmine	*Jasminum polyanthum*
Pieris	*Pieris japonica*
Ranunculus	*Ranunculus asiaticus* cv.
Rose	*Rosa* sp.
Sweet Pea	*Lathyrus odoratus* cv.

La Bayadère pp172–175

Anemone	*Anemone coronaria* cv.
Cymbidium Orchid	*Cymbidium* sp.
Fig	*Ficus* sp.
Ligularia	*Ligularia* sp.
Magnolia	*Magnolia* sp.
Rose	*Rosa* sp.
Tulip	*Tulipa* sp.

Enchanted Garden Party pp176–181

Elephant's Ear	*Xanthosoma* sp.
Emerald Duke Philodendron	*Philodendron* 'Emerald Duke'
Hydrangea	*Hydrangea macrophylla* cv.
Magnolia	*Magnolia* sp.
Nepenthes	*Nepenthes* sp.
Ornamental Kale	*Brassica oleracea* Acephala Group
Peony	*Paeonia* sp.
Sweet William	*Dianthus barbatus* cv.

Peonies pp182–183

Peonies	*Paeonia* spp.

Architectural Magnolia pp184–191

Ajuga	*Ajuga* sp.
Anemone	*Anemone coronaria* cv.
Artichoke, Globe Artichoke	*Cynara cardunculus* cv.
Calla Lily	*Zantedeschia aethiopica*
Daphne	*Daphne odora*
Daphne	*Daphne odora* 'Alba'
Hellebore Rose	*Helleborus* sp.
Loquat	*Eriobotrya japonica*
Magnolia	*Magnolia figo*
Magnolia	*Magnolia* sp.
Magnolia	*Magnolia* x *soulangeana* cv.
Ornamental Kale	*Brassica oleracea* Acephala Group
Rose 'Creme de Menthe'	*Rosa* 'Creme de Menthe'
Rose	*Rosa* David Austen cv.
Rose	*Rosa* sp.
Tulip 'Queen of the Night'	*Tulipa* 'Queen of the Night'
Violet	*Viola odorata*

Magnolias pp192–193

Magnolias	*Magnolia* spp.

Dreamy Barossa pp194–197

Blue Gum	*Eucalyptus* sp.
Carnation	*Dianthus barbatus* cv.
Olive	*Olea europaea*
Peony	*Paeonia* sp.
Rose	*Rosa* sp.
Western Australian	
Red Flowering Gum/Ficifolia Gum	*Corymbia ficifolia*

Fecund Canoe pp198–203

Amaranthus	*Amaranthus caudatus*
Bracken Fern	*Pteridium esculentum*
Carnation 'Green Trick'	*Dianthus barbatus* 'Green Trick'
Carnation	*Dianthus barbatus* cv.
Cymbidium Orchid	*Cymbidium* sp.
Echeveria	*Echeveria* sp.
Elephant's Ear	*Xanthosoma* sp.
Hydrangea	*Hydrangea macrophylla* cv.

LANTERN

Published by the Penguin Group
Penguin Group (Australia)
250 Camberwell Road, Camberwell, Victoria 3124, Australia
(a division of Pearson Australia Group Pty Ltd)
Penguin Group (USA) Inc.
375 Hudson Street, New York, New York 10014, USA
Penguin Group (Canada)
90 Eglinton Avenue East, Suite 700, Toronto, Canada ON M4P 2Y3
(a division of Pearson Penguin Canada Inc.)
Penguin Books Ltd
80 Strand, London WC2R 0RL England
Penguin Ireland
25 St Stephen's Green, Dublin 2, Ireland
(a division of Penguin Books Ltd)
Penguin Books India Pvt Ltd
11 Community Centre, Panchsheel Park, New Delhi – 110 017, India
Penguin Group (NZ)
67 Apollo Drive, Rosedale, North Shore 0632, New Zealand
(a division of Pearson New Zealand Ltd)
Penguin Books (South Africa) (Pty) Ltd
24 Sturdee Avenue, Rosebank, Johannesburg 2196, South Africa

Penguin Books Ltd, Registered Offices: 80 Strand, London, WC2R 0RL, England
First published by Penguin Group (Australia), 2011

1 3 5 7 9 10 8 6 4 2

Text copyright © Saskia Havekes 2011
Photographs copyright © Andrew Lehmann 2011
The moral right of the author has been asserted

Design by Arielle Gamble © Penguin Group (Australia)
Cover photograph by Andrew Lehmann
Author photograph by Andrew Lehmann
Typeset in Goudy 9.25/ 13.75pt by Post Pre-press Group, Brisbane, Queensland
Colour reproduction by Splitting Image, Clayton, Victoria
Printed and bound in China by 1010 Printing International Ltd

National Library of Australia
Cataloguing-in-Publication data:

Havekes, Saskia.
Grandiflora stories / Saskia Havekes; Andrew Lehmann.
1st ed.
ISBN: 9781921382222 (hbk.)
Grandiflora (Firm)
Flower arrangement – Pictorial works.
Floral decorations – Pictorial works.
Lehmann, Andrew.
745.92

penguin.com.au

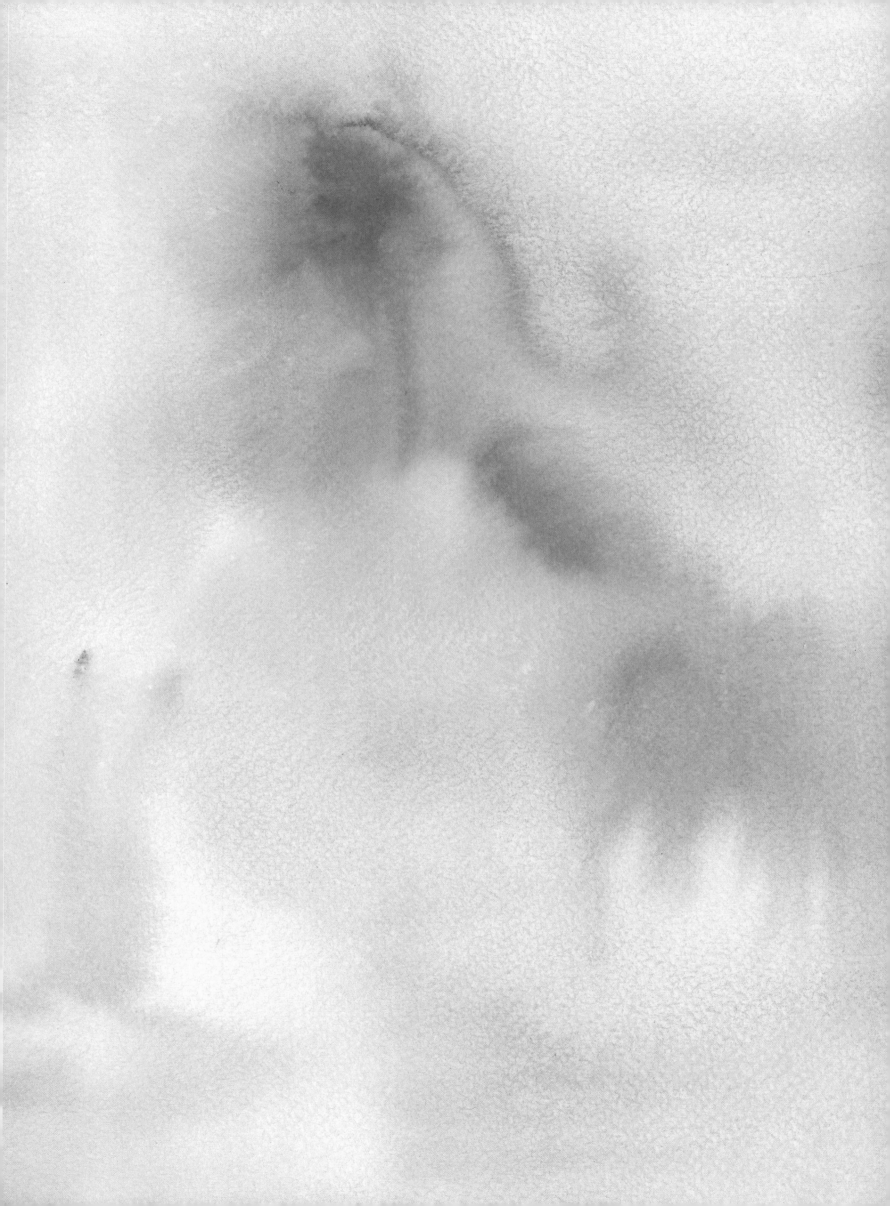